DOWN
BUT
NOT OUT

BECOMING A SIGNIFICANT
LEADER AT HOME

KIMUNYA MUGO

WestBow
PRESS
A DIVISION OF THOMAS NELSON

WestBow Press books may be ordered through booksellers or by contacting:

WestBow Press
A Division of Thomas Nelson
1663 Liberty Drive
Bloomington, IN 47403
www.westbowpress.com
1 (866) 928-1240

Because of the dynamic nature of the Internet, any web addresses or links contained in this book may have changed since publication and may no longer be valid. The views expressed in this work are solely those of the author and do not necessarily reflect the views of the publisher, and the publisher hereby disclaims any responsibility for them.

Any people depicted in stock imagery provided by Thinkstock are models, and such images are being used for illustrative purposes only.
Certain stock imagery © Thinkstock.

Unless otherwise noted, Scriptures are taken from the Holy Bible, New International Version®, NIV®. Copyright © 1973, 1978, 1984, 2011 by Biblica, Inc.™ Used by permission of Zondervan. All rights reserved worldwide. www.zondervan.com The "NIV" and "New International Version" are trademarks registered in the United States Patent and Trademark Office by Biblica, Inc.™ All rights reserved.

http://www.leadbychoice.co
Twitter: @KimunyaMugo
Facebook: KimunyaMugo

Cover design: Kimunya Mugo

ISBN: 978-1-4908-1533-6 (sc)
ISBN: 978-1-4908-1535-0 (hc)
ISBN: 978-1-4908-1534-3 (e)

Library of Congress Control Number: 2013921029

Printed in the United States of America.

WestBow Press rev. date: 11/21/2013

What others are saying

"Authentic and Transparent! Kimunya Mugo, in *Down But Not Out*, brings his incredible story to life in becoming a significant leader at home. Recognizing that home is where it starts, he delivers a roadmap to creating a legacy that any person would seek. A must read for any parent that desires to empower their children to live a life of significance despite the challenges that life throws at us every day."

—**Barry Smith**, *Building What Matters www. buildingwhatmatters.com*

"Like any good parent, Kimunya teaches you through his own touching stories and experiences. His upbringing in the majestic African savanna - in the shadow of My Kenya, provides a stark contrast to the struggles and heartache that Kimunya overcame to become the leader he is today."

—**Todd Nielsen**, *The Execution Expert, www.ToddNielsen.com*

"By the empowering of God and the responsibility that comes with personal leadership, there is nothing that cannot be done where forgiveness is the premise. Kimunya shares intimately, is candid and boldly states the importance of such values being first instilled by parents training their children to grow in 'wisdom, stature and favour with God and man'. The gem, captured in his own life story, is that where there are lapses in the training, hope still exists."

—**Michael Oyier**, *Psychologist and Media Practitioner, Founder and Director at Serenity Life Coaching, Nairobi Kenya*

"*Down But Not Out* comes from the heart of a man seeking for truth, one who is courageously pursuing to be a better leader, father and husband. A man who has a conviction about what he is doing. A man who deliberately moves out to do what he believes."

—**Peter Kisaka,** *Founder, Destiny Consult, Kampala Uganda*

Harriette, Tinashe, Tatenda, and Tumelo

The center of my universe…

My love and appreciation for you are more than words can describe. You definitely make my life more worth living.

"It is easier to build strong children than to repair broken men."

—Frederick Douglas

Contents

Foreword

A man named David O. McKay made one of the most profound statements about leadership, family, and success when he said, "No other success can compensate for failure in the home."

As a seeker of wisdom, and a writer, speaker, and consultant on leadership and execution, I feel overjoyed that Kimunya has chosen to write and teach on an aspect of leadership that I have failed to, for he has written about the most important leader that exists in the world.

This leader does not rule over a country, instead they preside over a home. They don't make policies and procedures for efficiencies sake; they set boundaries and limits for character's sake. They don't have board meetings, they have rituals. They don't do what is convenient, they do what is right. They don't work for money, they serve and they lead, for the value of a life. This leader holds the title of Father, or that of Mother.

In a world in which wrong influences crowd into children's minds and parents are pulled in a thousand directions, we need leaders at home that realize the importance of their role. We need leaders that make leadership in the home - the most important position they will ever hold.

Like any good parent, Kimunya teaches you through his own touching stories and experiences. His upbringing in the majestic African savanna - in the shadow of My Kenya, provides a stark contrast to the struggles and heartache that Kimunya overcame to become the leader he is today.

The six lessons that Kimunya teaches in this book apply to families throughout the globe. As you read his wonderful account, you might smile, you might laugh, you might even cry; but above all - take it in, ponder the lessons, and apply the six valuable steps on leadership in the home.

You can be the most important leader in the world, at least in your child's world. Next to that, nothing else really matters.

~Todd Nielsen - The Execution Expert

Todd is the author of *It's All About Execution: Transform Your Organization by Creating a Culture of 'Getting Things Done'* and *Managing For Execution: The Art of Getting Results from Others.*
www.ToddNielsen.com

Preface

This book came about as I searched for a way to find healing for my wounded heart. I had been blessed with an awesome family: a loving wife and great kids. Yet, I still felt like I had a big void in my heart that couldn't be filled by anything that I tried. Finally, I discovered that all along I yearned to be fully appreciated and loved by my Dad.

For most of my life, I had wondered why my father had hardly affirmed me as his son. Why had he chosen to be consistently away from home for extended chunks of time? Why is it that he wasn't there for me through the different seasons of my life? Is it that I was such a "nobody" that he would care less that his son was growing and needed his father, a mentor and a guide? This left me with a deep-seated anger and acrid bitterness at his absence, both which I had held on for thirty years!

The more I came to grips with what was in my heart, the more I got a conviction that I needed to forgive my Dad. Without this, I could not move forward in my quest to become a better husband, father and leader wherever I was.

It all began with a two-page letter to my Dad. I was writing to tell him that I had forgiven him for not being there for me. For leaving a feeling in me that I was unwanted. Soon, the two pages turned into a chapter, and before long this book was born.

Four years before this book was conceived, my wife and I were privileged to facilitate our first parenting classes. It was clear that most participants were eager to learn, inasmuch as some seemed a tad sceptical as to the class' benefits. The twelve-week classes are designed to help and equip parents with practical skills, discipline "how-to's", guide them on building strong parent-child relationships, and ultimately, empower parents to take full leadership in their homes.

Around the same time, I began to explore gaps in my quest for leadership. I studied other leaders and scoured hundreds of leadership resources (books, videos, podcasts, websites, and blogs). I started writing a blog to help me internalize the leadership lessons I was learning.

This book, therefore, culminated my journey to forgive and opened up a gift for me to share with others. I hope this will be a first step to guide them through past issues that limits their current potential to lead. My hope is that my pain and healing will help many to grow and become better leaders at home.

Acknowledgements

To Harriette, my precious friend and wife for your amazing love, encouragement, and support. The good book was right... "He who finds a wife finds a good thing." And to our awesome three children, you have taught me the essentials of leadership at home. You inspire me to become a better leader, and to serve community even more.

Todd Nielsen, a selfless friend who inspired and supported me through the journey of self-discovery. You provided me with a platform to express myself to the world, for which I will forever be thankful.

To my contributors who brought some real-life examples of what leading at home is all about: W.P. Kamau, Muthoni Njomba, Kasera Kadondi, Evelyn Wangari, and Peter Mutua.

Anzaya and Mbithe, you taught us the ropes of parenting, by word and deed. You are amazing people!

Mumo and Irene, for guiding Harriette and I when we began our journey as a family. The two of you have been an inspiration in many ways.

My parents, Christine, David, and Pricilla... you have been pillars of strength and beacons of hope. And to Francis, with you I came to appreciate what it means to forgive.

Introduction

Leaders must have a Vision, the ability to think about or plan the future with imagination or wisdom. It is what Chapter 1, *Lead With Intent*, opens with. Together, we explore why it is important for leaders to be out in the frontline. As they do this, they understand what threats (and enemies) their followers are likely to come across. I take us through my journey to finding healing the pain that had left my heart wounded, and my opportunity at a second chance at life. You do not need some special conditions to set you off on your quest, you can start in whichever situation you are in and you'll be off to setting your family values.

In Chapter 2, *Broken Windows*, we begin to appreciate why as a leader you must make deliberate decisions and the hazards that you will need to navigate through. However, you will soon discover that there may be some tough issues from the past that you'll have to deal with. As this happens, then the joy and challenges of laying down boundaries will become apparent. These boundaries help you to keep the good in and the bad out as you work towards providing your followers with an identity.

Chapter 3 is *Courage to Change*. It is about taking responsibility for the choices that you make. Taking on leadership comes with change, and change has a whole set of challenges that come with it. Mediocrity is one such challenge, the urge to remain within your comfort zone and not pushing on to the next level. However, with a dose of inspiration from guidelines herein, overcoming these challenges will become a reality. As you lead your family, we will walk through why the relationship between parents is a cornerstone to the development of children and the family.

One of the hallmarks of a leader is his or her ability to journey together. Chapter 4 espouses *Presence Rocks!* It's about you the leader being out in the frontline with your troops. As your followers experience your courage and strength, they gain confidence as they also discover who they are. Follow through and you will find yourself creating your family identity. But you will need to watch out for discipline issues and how to tackle them. We close this chapter with working through how creating precious memories with your family and followers can work wonders during periods or indiscipline and self-discovery.

In Chapter 5, *Taking Stock*, you explore why it is important to always pause and understand where you are in every stage of your leadership. You will acquire knowledge on how to build a healthy culture. Teaching and inspiration becomes a lighthouse for your followers. You will be able to guide them on how to think and be thought leaders to people around them. You will also need to understand how to manage behavior change in your followers, and have fun in "tackles, cuddles and kisses".

As you practice the first five chapters of this book, it is important to remember that a leader exists in a community. Chapter 6 takes you through the joy of giving to others. Dream big and *Pay It Forward* as it not only builds your character, it helps you grow a strong community around you. You will engage with other individuals who have chosen to take leadership of their families and lives, with very inspiring outcomes.

I welcome you to engage with this content with an open mind and expectant heart. My prayer is that you will be transformed and enjoy your leadership, even through those curve balls life may pitch your way every now and then.

Prologue

"Every morning in Africa, a gazelle wakes up. It knows it must run faster than the fastest lion or it will be killed. Every morning a lion wakes up. It knows it must outrun the slowest gazelle or it will starve to death. It doesn't matter if you are a lion or a gazelle, when the sun comes up, you'd better be running."
—**Herb Caen,** *former columnist at the San Francisco Chronicle*

At seven years old, life held unlimited possibilities. I enjoyed the present with the sort of enthusiasm only a child has, and the future looked amazing. When I was young, I could not wait to grow up so that I could scale the heights of Mt. Kenya and enjoy the snow on its top. From my maternal grandparents' home, it was just five miles to the base of the mountain.

To the south of our home the wildebeests raced as they performed their well-orchestrated annual migration in the Maasai Mara.

Nearby, deep in the Great Rift Valley, the so-called cradle of mankind, I experienced years of unmatched beauty. Sunny Saturdays at our home were filled with the smell of fresh-mown grass and the orange splash of Mexican marigold blossoms bordering our lawn. Muddy pools, tadpoles, the dismantling of grasshoppers, lollypops, and meat pies—oh what a life I had.

Each Saturday, my dad would bring out the lawn mower. The put-put of its tiny four-horsepower engine sent shivers down my spine. The anticipation, excitement… the simple prospect of spending time with Dad was overwhelming. The reward at the end was a large pile of cushiony new grass trimmings that I could frolic in. With a mighty whoop, I would charge at the pile, then just as I was about to hit it, I would catapult my lithe, sinewy muscles into a summersault.

After hours of sheer ecstasy, my mum would call out to my brother and me to come indoors. It was bath time. What a killjoy we thought she was! My exploits in the grass would yield its dividends in endless itching when the bathwater hit the grass cuts. The itching was a worthy price to pay for the fun, and for having my daddy's company.

Dad was very good with his hands. He could fix anything at home, from our transistor radio to a broken pipe. I loved rifling through his amazing stamp collection, as it was my window to foreign lands. Occasionally, he would make major repairs on his beloved Volkswagen Kombi van. These were "smooth" days of grease, oil, and sweat.

Such intimate time with my dad made me feel connected to him. The fact that he allowed me to tinker with parts of the car had a massive impact on me. It meant that he trusted me enough not to break stuff. It was a mark of approval, not only of my abilities, but also as a man. The exertion of tearing the car apart would open up a ravenous hunger deep in the caverns of my poor stomach. However, nothing would tear me from my dad's side. I would push on until my hands were quivering with fatigue. Only then could I tear myself from my dad to the welcoming aroma of my mom's sumptuous meals.

I was born in a town filled with spectacular nature; the outdoors was the place to be. My dad frequently drove us down for picnics at the world famous Lake Nakuru National Park. The sea of pink flamingos was blinding to the eye, and a beautiful sight to behold in contrast to the hundreds of barking baboons, whose bare and raw-looking behinds only served to increase my hatred of them.

Camping in the park afforded me the luxury of baths in the clear river. Bathing was done when the sun was way up in the sky, as the waters could be shockingly frigid. On occasion, I would venture out to a small waterfall for a heavenly shower. The only tricky bit was that I had to navigate through some slippery, wet rocks. This was also a favorite route for the resident troop of baboons, who would also seek out the pleasures of the same waterfall.

Life with Dad was just great!

During the Easter season, three things came together that made every boy my age tingle with excitement. First, school was out for a month… no math, grammar, or science! This season also marked the rebirth of life, as seed was sown into the freshly plowed land. Soon the fields would be covered in green sprouts, madly competing for sun and space. Pumpkins, maize, beans, potatoes, and an assortment of vegetables would sprout like green fingers out of the rich, moist dirt.

Second was the celebration of Christ's death and resurrection during the Easter weekend. The plays and stories always left me awestruck. How could a man be so brutally executed, yet rise from the dead and forgive his executioners? The implications always left me dumbfounded. It never ceased to amaze me how this event could be dramatized every year, yet I still found myself yearning for more of this man.

The third—and the most exciting of them all in the eyes of a rambunctious young boy—was a throaty, thunderous, mud-filled meeting of man and machine: for about five days, the Safari Rally rolled into town and reigned supreme. Time stood still! It was second to no other event on the annual calendar of any testosterone-filled male. It was a time of fun and travel out to the bush in pursuit of motorsport.

Weeks before the rally cars came into town, all the boys my age would energetically construct their own rally cars. Using salvaged wire fencing cables bent into shape and held together with strips of old inner tire tubes, we would construct amazing models of the actual rally cars. Once our cars were finished, the race route was mapped out. The route was outfitted with race marshals, service points, and service cars, just like the real rally that would soon be on its way. For a whole weekend, we would race all over the neighborhood. Many other boys across the country were under a similar spell. We had fun, fought, made up, went to sleep, and repeated it all again the next day. For that short period, boys ruled! I could see the raw hunger lurking beneath every male skin I walked past.

The childlike, untamed excitement that bound my heart to my dad's defied age and size. I knew Dad felt the same beastly need to pursue the rally cars just as we boys did. The excitement of these two thrills threatened to cause my heart to leap out of my chest with unspeakable joy.

Life with my dad around was awesome. Upon being asked what I wanted to become, I'd blurt out without hesitation, "When I grow up, I want to be like Daddy!". For dramatic effect, I would thrust out my skinny, rib-decked chest in a display of boyish pride. My father was my pillar of refuge, the conqueror of anything that crossed his path. Life, I thought, was full of reckless unrestraint and a future as grand as the mind could imagine. Life was good. That was the powerhouse my father was to me.

However, a long nightmare was brewing. Unbeknownst to me, my father was about to be heartlessly torn away from me. Soon, he was transferred to a different location and had to move away to a town far from home. This would take him away from his family… away from me. Some years, he would be gone for up to eleven months at a time. It was a bad dream that was to last nearly two decades.

During this fateful year when my life would start to spin on its head, the car that was the talk of the Safari Rally was the Dodge Ram Charger, a monster of a vehicle that dwarfed all other rally cars. The rumble of its engine was like that of a mad buffalo: primal, awe-inspiring. As intimidating as this monster vehicle was, it did not compare to how much life seemed suddenly to intimidate me. I had to man-up up fast. With my dad away, I was suddenly thrust into the alpha male position as the eldest of four children. Crippling fear welled up in my heart. How would I make it in life without my father around?

However, as the years went by, I slowly grew into a young man; and as I did, I dreamt of becoming a better man than my father was. This was driven by Dad's long periods of absence from home that had left me disillusioned about my identity as well as his love for his family. My bewilderment was how a man who claimed to care chose to stay away from me.

With time, I started to develop a vision for my future. It was driven by my pent-up anger against the perceived abandonment by my Dad. My bitterness for him had grown to such proportions that any thought of him caused a massive dose of adrenaline to shoot through me. I would be filled with rage. I was faced with daunting challenges and terrible trials with a deep yearning for a mature man to guide me through life.

As I sought my life's purpose, I sought after role models to fill the void left behind by my Dad's absence. Some helped me somewhat while others just didn't care. I was not systematic in my quest. However, unbeknownst to me, I had begun a journey toward the discovery of the *six keys* that would open up the door to leadership in my own home. It led me to forgive my Dad, brought healing to my aching heart. I was slowly working towards becoming the best man and father I could possibly be. And nothing would get in my way.

1. Lead with Intent

If you have a vision, you will eventually attract the right strategy. If you don't have a clear vision, no strategy will save you.
—*Michael Hyatt*

Vision |noun| • the ability to think about or plan the future with imagination or wisdom[1]

Leaders (and Fathers) Must Have a Vision

At nine, I had my spiritual awakening when I committed my life to my Maker, a commitment I made with my mother by my side. Right there, on the dirt floor of our living room, I bent my knee and asked God to take over my heart and life. That day, I gained a friend greater than any I had yet to meet or ever will.

At the same age, I discovered a wonderful horse called Black Beauty. *Black Beauty* is a novel by English author Anna Sewell written in 1877. It was composed in the last years of her life, during which she remained in her house as an invalid. While forthrightly teaching animal welfare, it also teaches how to treat people with kindness, sympathy, and respect. That year, *Black Beauty* was being serialized on national television. I must have been the only boy in my class who was watching the amazing production of this wonderful classic. *Superman*, *Spider-Man*, and the *Fantastic 4* were the rave with all the other boys. I watched those heroes too, but they all paled in comparison to my beloved Black Beauty.

In the story, Black Beauty is initially a carriage horse for wealthy people, but when he "breaks his knees" (he develops scars on his knees after a bad fall), he is no longer considered presentable enough and is given much harder work. As he passes through the hands of a series of owners—some cruel, some kind—he always tries his best to serve those humans regardless of the circumstance.[2]

The reasons I was starstruck by this majestic horse were two-fold. First, he was going through misery similar to my own. I was this scrawny, skinny kid desperately trying to find out what my identity was. The second reason was his resilience. Black Beauty continued to perform good deeds even though he was repeatedly mistreated. I, too, knew suffering; I was constantly taken advantage of by very close relatives who manipulated me into silence thereafter. I was learning from Black Beauty that negative circumstances did not have to make me a negative person.

As my grandparents lived closer to my school, I would on occasion spend the weekdays with them. They owned a black-and-white television set, a valuable treasure for me. We did not have a television—nor electricity and running water—back home. When I was spending time over at my grandparents' house, Thursday's were all but a race. After school was out in the afternoon, I would run across the two miles that bridged the school and their house as fast as my sinewy legs would carry me.

From that television series, one conversation became embedded in my mind to this day. It was a conversation that Black Beauty's master, John, had with Black Beauty: "God has given men reason, by which they could find out things for themselves, but He has given animals knowledge which did not depend on reason, and which was much more prompt and perfect in its way, and by which they have often saved the lives of men."[3]

If only my father could have opened his eyes to the knowledge that his growing son craved for his presence and that his family longed for him to be home more. But I guess his mind and heart were not focused on growing closer to his family. As long as he provided for us, everything else apparently seemed insignificant. How wrong he was. His entire family but him saw that he had all his priorities wrong side up.

It never ceases to amaze me how our existence can become devoid of life when we don't have a vision. We are buffeted by the battles that rage inside our minds and the old wounds that tear at our hearts. We grope precariously through life's maze. Our forward progress is informed by our past; when we don't take time to fully appreciate where we are coming from, it becomes very difficult to set a vision for our future.

Broken Trust

Nine was also the age when my life was opened up to bitterness. This bitterness was so intense that it very nearly eclipsed my emotional, social, and spiritual potential. I had periods of savage resentment at the life I had been thrust into and times so bleak that living did not make any sense. This was triggered by a series of seemingly unrelated events that could only have been committed by a person running on highly refined evil. It was a season of emotional, physical, and mental torture. Other horrible factors, like overt alcohol consumption and covert substance abuse, were subtle to begin with, but in the end, the outcome on my life was just as devastating as Hurricane Katrina was on New Orleans.

For years, these events would keep my family torn apart. Pain ran deep while dreams were shattered and lives were devastated forever. This "family" broke a cardinal piece of the code that holds any relationship together: trust. The broken trust violated all accountability, predictability, and dependability. There was no one I could lay claim to as a leader.

Apart from my mother and paternal grandmother, I cannot recall anyone else in the family that I could trust. These two women were solid in their faith in God and cared for all of us deeply. Apart from them, for most of my life I did not know which adult members of my family I could place my trust in. This includes my father. For over twenty-five years, I lived a life filled with a bagful of bile for the man.

During those terrible childhood years, it felt like I was walking through a rough neighborhood, constantly looking over my shoulder, not knowing where the muggers were hiding or when they would strike. I felt unsafe. This was a painful existence. No child should have to block off a part of his or her life in a bid to find peace within.

It would be years until life changed for the better. I married the most wonderful woman any man could dream of; a great family was born. A handsome son and two beautiful daughters soon completed the big picture. However, even this eventual great fortune only provided an escape from a past dotted with dark times of struggle, pain, poverty, and need. It did not close the old wounds. I would have paid anything—everything—to forget and totally obliterate this history.

Enemy Within

Initially there was excitement as Dad would come home every Friday laden with the types of goodies every kid craved, such as toy cars, candy, and new clothes. He would be gone Monday to Friday and come home over the weekend. As time progressed, so did the distance between home and work. The visits became even more spaced out, to just a weekend each month. There were no more of our father-son activities; his existence in my life deteriorated into a drab routine. When Dad was home, too many other "important" things occupied him, and he had no time for his son. I was devastated.

Some years before, my parents had invited an uncle to live with us as he completed his high school education. It was great to have him around. He would give me piggyback rides and hoist me up on his shoulders to my delirious delight.

Once my father left, this uncle somewhat filled the vacuum left behind. At first, all was well. That was until a very dark side of this great uncle reared its ugly head, and our relationship broke down completely. My vision of having a significant male-figure evaporated like a mist in the midday sun. My young, innocent life was gradually shattered. There was no one to talk to about the things that happened while Mum was not home and my father was far away—sitting in a bar somewhere deep into the night, drinking his life away.

Threats, fear, and rejection played hard on my fragile young mind. Nothing was said or disclosed; it seemed too dangerous for me. I had been intimidated into submission. Yet the shame was slowly eating me from within. I had to unceremoniously suck it up and man-up. I had to protect myself the only way I knew how: grow a callous ring to guard my precious heart. My mind and my emotions were exposed and armed like ticking time bombs. I had to block out all the pain, all the hurt, all the shame. I wondered if this could prove to be a cost too heavy to pay, a burden too heavy to bear. Would I explode at those who had let me down, like an angry volcano erupting into a fiery spray of magmatic discharge?

I felt like my family had been pushed to a precipice. Like debris from a shipwreck, my family members slowly drifted along, strangers living under the same roof. The only identity we shared with each other was a common surname and the need to survive. The adults in the family were too proud to admit everything had completely broken down and the center did not hold anymore.

It was like there was an invisible enemy that was slowly eating away at this basic building block of community from within itself. Sanity, direction, hope, and mentorship were lacking. Selfishness abounded; it seemed to have a vise grip on everyone's soul, driving people to the misplaced need to satisfy themselves before their family. Everything else, including their children and spouses, became secondary. This virus was driving the rot we experienced all around us. The enemy within, it seems, may have been too large a dragon to slay. It's possible we might not have appreciated the hurt our families had been exposed to.

Hurt brought with it issues of self-esteem and appreciation of who I was as a person. Worthless, filthy and of no value is how I felt. I became more reclusive. In order to try to gain any significance, I worked hard on my grades in school. Every good grade on my report card brought with it some praise, and this gave me the impression that I was accepted. But the more I tried, the greater the sense of hopelessness I felt within me.

For many years I lived my life feeling like an empty shell. At the back of my mind, some intensely stressful questions lingered. Where was my Dad when I was going through all this difficulty? Why could he not spend enough time with me to "uncover" the pain that my body was being subjected to and the torment that ravaged my young mind? I felt very helpless and lost. The more I spiraled into this dark vortex, the deeper my hatred and anger towards my Dad became.

In the prologue to this book, I described a scenario that is pertinent to maturity: *initiation* is a very deliberate voyage through tough, challenging lessons that are meant to help the initiate to understand and discover who he is. Without this experience, a person may end up running around, chasing his tail, trying to establish his real self and worth. However, pride and fear may cause others not to admit that they are hurting, that they are mortally wounded and need urgent care.

Writing this book was a way for me to deal with the emotional wounds I had received from my father, who had never cared enough to be physically present for me when I was a young, vulnerable boy growing up. This was the first step of a grueling journey towards forgiveness and to free my heart, which was engulfed in bitterness. This came at a price though. I made many mistakes as I blindly groped for guidance. Sometimes I landed in bad company and I was misled. It was in this confusion that I decided to seek knowledge. I read many books to help me build a positive self-image.

Many years later, my wife bought me a book that I had promptly shelved under the "to-read" section. When I finally got round to reading the book, it opened up a whole new world to me. I could now appreciate why some thread of hopelessness still lingered, even after I had created a vision and pursuing it with all my heart. The book was *Wild at Heart* by John Eldredge.

Healing Wounds

In this book, I found this powerful passage:

"God is fiercely committed to you, to the restoration and release of your masculine heart. But a wound that goes unacknowledged and unwept is a wound that cannot heal. A wound you think you deserved is a wound that cannot heal. That is why Brennan Manning says, 'The spiritual life begins with the acceptance of the wounded self.' Really? How can that be? The reason is simple: 'Whatever is denied cannot be healed.' But that's the problem, you see. Most men deny their wound–deny it happened, deny that it hurt certainly, deny that it's shaping the way they live today. And God's initiation of a man must take a very cunning course; a course that feels very odd, even cruel. He will wound us in the very place where we have been wounded."[4] *[sic]*

Reading that completely challenged my thinking and refined my direction. I had to start all over again, I had to debunk my own belief that I was that by not letting myself be vulnerable enough to accept that I carried with me a shipload of wounds, I was being a real man. Once I began to understand and accept this, the tears came; I could not hold them back. The painful wounds tore open; memories came back to me like an uncontrollable flood. I would have expected the tears to bring with them a dark grey cloud from the past. Yet, surprisingly, as the tears flowed, I experienced a break in the clouds. My soul felt like it was bathing in a warm, soothing light. I sensed the healing had just begun.

Second Chances

One particular Friday a decade before my encounter with *Wild at Heart* became a prominent mile-marker in my life. On this day, I saw my life flash before my mind's eye. It all began with a simple night out for dinner at a local restaurant with some friends. I had ordered a juicy pepper steak that was accompanied by some delicious, aromatic rice. As we enjoyed our dinner, a grain of rice went the wrong way. After a few coughs and a heaving chest, the coast was clear... or so I thought.

The cough resumed on my way home, but I was able to have a good night of rest. Friday morning was bright and sunny as I prepared to go to work. The niggling cough was still there, but I did not think much of it. However, after a few hours at the office, I decided to go see a doctor and have it checked out. Around the same time, I had an appointment to meet a good friend who worked on the same campus with me. He was buying a car and wanted me to be a witness to the transaction. So there I was, lucky to have a ride to the hospital. We completed the transaction and he dropped me off. I went over to the doctor's office, did my paperwork and waited in turn at the reception area.

Less than five minutes later, I started to feel very strange. I could not really explain what was going on with my body. I am the athletic type, and besides the occasional knocks, sprained joints, and the common cold, I have never had major problems with my health. I walked over to the receptionist and informed her that I was not feeling too well. In the few minutes it took to arrange for me to be ushered onto a bed in an open room, my body started to behave in a strange manner.

I could feel numbness creeping up my limbs, I struggled to remove my shoes to get onto the bed, my fingers were not responding well to my brain's signals. I was like a misfiring engine. Three minutes later, I started to lose the feeling in my feet. It was as if a giant syringe was sucking the life out from my limbs! This was scaring the living daylights out of me. Within minutes, the numbness had crept up all of my limbs and into my torso. My tongue felt full and heavy in my mouth and I started to slur my speech. My eyes felt heavy, like they do when I have gone for a full day without sleep. Yet I was fully conscious this entire time, even as the light in the room seemed to gradually dim.

Shortly, I heard a synchronized commotion in the room: muted voices of efficient nurses in action while a doctor prodded every part of my body, trying to establish what was going on. I could hear everything that was happening around me but I could not open my eyes to see, nor utter a single word to say how I was feeling. "Run a drip line, quick," I heard the doctor say in a clear, terse voice. As a line was run on one arm, a technician was drawing blood from the other. "Get the morphine ready now!"

As all this was going on, the most surreal thing happened, something akin to what happens in the movies, flashbacks. For two hours, scenes from my life sped through the darkness of my mind. I could visualize things I did as a child, experiences I had at very specific periods in my life. It was akin to an out-of-body experience. It was like someone had popped in a recording of my life and was rewinding it and playing it back again. I thought I was going to die any minute, and that God was asking me to make things right with Him before the candle of my life was finally snuffed out.

Suddenly, my body regained its sensation. It was not pleasant at all. You know that uncomfortable feeling of pins-and-needles you get in your leg or arm after it has been asleep? Extrapolate that to your whole body. It was as if a deranged acupuncturist and his mad cousins had been let loose on me! To say the least, it was very painful.

Finally, I was able to sit up. I could not believe what had just transpired. The preliminary tests showed nothing wrong with my body. No infections or injuries... nothing. A cocktail of drugs was prescribed and I was sent home with strict instructions to make sure I had complete rest. The following day, I went back to the hospital for another check-up. It was then that the doctor informed me that they had thought they were going to lose me during that crisis. That second check-up, and the blood results indicated that everything was normal.

Given another bite at the cherry, I had no choice but to firmly commit to developing a crystal-clear vision for my life. My living had to matter. I remember being drawn to this message:

"For whoever has will be given more, and they will have an abundance. Whoever does not have, even what they have will be taken from them." Matthew 25:29 (NIV)

Start Where You Are

When I was twelve years old, I made some rather bold (and perhaps potentially dangerous) decisions. I had to take control of my life and drive it to a bigger good. The first bold decision was that I would one day get married and have two children.

Later on in life, I realized that what I lay down for myself was one heck of a vision; one that common consent would have decreed was doomed to fail, mostly due to the mediocrity that surrounded me. Many in my extended family secretly—or so they thought—believed that my life would not amount to anything significant. This spurred me on. Not only did I make it through high school, but by God's grace and kindness and through much hard work, I became the first person in my family to earn a college degree, and a science one at that.

Another significant promise I made to myself was that I would make space in my life for my children, that when the time came, I would be available to roll with them in the grass, enjoy moments of silly jokes, and just as importantly, devote myself to loving their mother, my soul mate.

With careful thought, I began to plan how I would make my vision clearer and achievable. I read widely on personal development and prayed passionately for divine guidance. Slowly and steadily, my vision was all-but carved in granite, and I was determined to go to great lengths to make this happen!

No one would shake it; no amount of pressure was going to budge this ambition.

Building on this vision was in my sights when my wife and I went through our courtship. I realized even more that I had to step up and lead the change that would hopefully redeem my family tree. Again prayer came in handy here. My wife and I also sought the counsel of a mentor couple to help us navigate through the maze of our future marriage. These helped me tremendously as I wondered what steps I should take. Let us walk these steps, a journey whose final destination was years into the future. An adventurous spirit, fervent prayer, intense study and many lessons along the way guided these steps.

I suspect your journey will be just as adventurous. I do not promise the voyage will be easy, but always have this wisdom from Tuli Kupferberg at the back of your mind: "When patterns are broken, new worlds emerge."

Set Your Family Values

To guide my Family Vision, I started by setting the Values the vision would adhere to. These core values were: availability, discipline, honor, belonging (culture), and audacity.

When I was a small boy, my father was everything to me. However, one value he never espoused was to be fully available to his family. *Availability* is a Value that guides me to this day and is a key driver for how I prioritize my time. I am very deliberate about spending quality time with my family. My career and personal goals have to be in tandem with the value I place on being available for my family. This has had a remarkable effect on my family. I am able to build healthy relationships with my wife and children. The impact on our children is of special note here. As they grow older, they are displaying more confidence in their relationships not only with their peers, but with adults too. They take initiative in engaging in conversation.

Being available has additional benefits especially when any of our children are going through a period of low self-esteem or emotional turmoil. Because of our close relationship, they feel free to approach my wife or I for help and comfort. They have confidence in us and do not fear to display how vulnerable they feel. It also gives us the confidence that our children can confide what is in their hearts with us.

I do not remember any structure for discipline at home as a child. *Discipline* (order and focus) wasn't instilled as a value, rather meted out as a measure to keep my siblings and I on the "straight-and-narrow." The only time I remember my father mentioning anything to do with discipline was in reference to my schoolwork. I think the only reason I chose to remain disciplined was to avoid being on the receiving end of some painful experience. For my own family, discipline was going to be used as a way to cement my relationship with our children, and not as punishment. For this, my wife and I chose to learn all we could about parenting long before our first child was born. We attended parenting classes, sought advice from our mentors, and with time, chose to start coaching other parents over time. For discipline to be effective, a relationship has to exist in the present. In this case, it is important that both the parent and the child fully understand order and focus, including the consequences of ignoring the parameters therein. My wife and I also ensure that our children fully understand the consequences of indiscipline and what the remedial measures are. Discipline then becomes a Core Value of how the family relates, as members are able to stay within the bounds of healthy engagement.

Honor hardly existed in my family when I was growing up.

Apart from my mother and paternal grandmother, both of whom I regarded with great respect, I could hardly draw any sense of honor from the rest of my extended family. Everyone seemed to be focused more on self-enhancement than building up the rest of the family. Elders took advantage of the ignorance and innocence of younger members of the family to enrich themselves. I decided that honor was going to be redeemed in my own family; it was going to be a Core Value to be pursued

"Do I *belong*?" As a child this question constantly blighted my thoughts, recurring, like the sun, with every new day. It was difficult to find my bearing as to what role I played in my family. There was this constant feeling, like I was just passing through on my way to my real home. Later, however, I realized that we were suffering from a lack of a common collective of customs and behavior that were unique to our family. It would have given me a sense of belonging with the knowledge that as a unit, we had some distinctive features that made us stand out within the broader community. Why would I subject my wife and children to such deficiency? I made the decision that my family would have a strong culture to help us reach our Family Vision.

Finally, I chose *audacity* as an encompassing Value that was in the background of everything I did. I needed to take bold risks to protect and build my family's character, existence, and influence of the community around it. Unlike when I was growing up, I would not play into the status quo. I would do what was right for the sake of my family and help them to become positive influences wherever they were. For example, I chose not to have my career take priority over my family. It was paramount to have a balance between the time I had to spend in my career versus that which I invested in my family.

My good friend, Dr. Lyn Boyer, author of *Connect: Affective Leadership for Effective Results* provides us with some wonderful insight regarding the importance of solid values. First, she notes that *values guide action*. If we do not promote family or try to spend time with family members, then Family Values become secondary to our existence as a family unit. Acting in violation of stated values (and public values statements) feeds cynicism and mistrust. I have to live the values I have set out if my family is to follow through as well.

Secondly, relatives and the public judge a family's character by its members' actions. Unless family members fully understand and embrace a values statement and live by the principles it suggests, the values statement is worthless. These Family Values also help the family to set the limits within which they operate. As the leader of my family, I need to constantly communicate these boundaries to both my family and those we interact with. These boundaries define what is permissible and what isn't.

Her third argument is that values generate emotions and culture. The void that was left by the lack of solid values in my family as I grew up left me feeling vulnerable to the world around me. That feeling evoked a lot of anger and bitterness in me. Confusion, frustration, and fear surfaced when I could not understand why many of those I loved did not appreciate the need of a value-system. I did not have a culture I could turn to for direction and this left me disillusioned. However, I did have some values and positive culture passed down to me by my mother and this helped somewhat. But my Dad not being around, and my mother thus having to shoulder extra responsibility, affected my mother's ability to teach me and lead me.

I hated my father for his abandonment.

2. Broken Windows

"The indispensible first step to getting the things you want out of life is this: decide what you want."
—*Ben Stein*

Decision |noun| • a resolution reached after consideration

Leaders Must Make Decisions

Being a leader at home is a complex affair; at times it can be downright frustrating. Children grow through different stages at a breathtaking rate. No sooner have you hit the pit stop than you have to head back out to the speedway mighty fast. It does not matter whether you have had time to refuel or change your tires, life must go on.

The hurried pace of modern life may blur your vision for the minute issues and problems that repeatedly crop up. It becomes comforting to park these issues off the track, to be sorted out later. The issues pile up, and soon you are in deep trouble! To understand where you are headed into, you must acknowledge the environment you exist in:

- Who are your friends?
- What inspires your choices?
- Do you have clearly articulated goals for your life?

Appreciating the context in which you exist becomes your launch pad to the next big choice: you may wallow in the muck, or you can work to identify the factors that led you into the muck and then begin to free yourself from it. In life, we have to make tough decisions as we respond to the three questions above.

One decision may be to reduce the amount of time we spend on our work commitments and invest more time in our immediate families (wife and children). Another may involve taking a pay cut in the short term to ensure that you develop solid relationships with our family in the long term. This may also require you to seriously evaluate your friendships and sever those that compromise other significant relationships. Note the long-term rewards that will come if people do make the hard (but positive) choice of prioritizing family over everything.

Hazards

Like hairline cracks in a bridge, my family relations when I was growing up were a disaster waiting to happen. The bridge was still intact, but for how long could we stand on it before it collapsed under us? There was a high level of discord and our family was going through great strife. If such tension existed within the broader community, journalists and pundits and intellectuals would have taken note and searched in despair for solutions. My family was riddled with many signs that all was not well. It resembled a building in the neighborhood that was riddled with broken windows.

In 1982, criminologists James Q. Wilson and George Kelling introduced the Broken Windows Theory. Their premise was that if there was a building with a few broken windows and the windows were not repaired, over time the most probable outcome was that vandals would break a few more windows. With time, if the building continued in disrepair and decay, the vandals might eventually break into the building and become squatters.

The same would apply to trash on a sidewalk. All it takes is a few people to litter and for it not to be cleaned up. People passing through the same street may perceive the accumulating litter as a license to leave their trash there. Eventually, the attitude that allowed for these unkempt streets might spread to other social ills, leading to muggings or cars being broken into.

Malcolm Gladwell aptly demonstrates this in his book *Tipping Point*[5] as the 'Power of Context' concerning how epidemics spread. He argues that epidemics don't just suddenly occur. They are the product of closely-knit factors that, when added together, explode into a major event—even something so initially innocuous as one piece of trash on the street leading bit-by-bit to larger urban decay.

Broken windows characterized the decaying walls around my family life. Some signs—such as a previously independent boy suddenly seeking more and more attention, desperate to be noticed—were very subtle and hardly apparent to those barely paying attention. Other signs were as evident as a lighthouse against a pitch-black sky. My grandfather would come home drunk as a skunk, making unintelligent conversation in the presence of his grandchildren. There was also the *khat*-chewing uncle who was constantly on edge from the high he derived from chewing the leafy stimulant. It seemed like everyone just accepted these things as status quo, as normal occurrences of life. However, for the young children growing up in this family, this was way too much unnecessary exposure to the darker sides of life. These dangerous stimulations of the senses would lead to negative results such as truancy and substance abuse for some of those children in the future.

I realized that I could not win the race to the bottom. A mighty big crowd had already beaten me! In his wisdom, Martin Luther King Jr. had said the following, "As my sufferings mounted I soon realized that there were two ways in which I could respond to my situation—either to react with bitterness or seek to transform the suffering into a creative force. I decided to follow the latter course." *[sic]*

I desperately needed to break away from this mediocrity that had become my daily grind. With too many skeptics around me, it was time to shut off all the negative voices that sought to control me. I wanted to run away and immediately be free, but also knew that I needed to grow up first. In my free time, I immersed myself in volunteer work and youth activities at my church. This kept me occupied with positive influences and helped me grow not only physically, but also spiritually and also a well-balanced member of society.

Finally, my journey away from home began when I was admitted into college. It was at least a six-hour journey one way. I would be away from home for at least sixteen weeks at a time with a two-to-three-week break in between. During the time I was away from home, I started to rebuild myself from ground up.

Elephant in the Room

It would take several years before I began to feel any sense of self-confidence creep back into my severely mutilated soul. My system was terribly broken, so much so that it required serious fixing. I urgently needed to shift from thinking about problems to talking about possibilities. I had to accept that there was an elephant in the room with me. I urgently needed to address the demons that were wreaking havoc in my head.

With no point of reference or guidance from any male authority figure, all I could do was to develop a Vision. Slowly, I began to develop a vivid, positive picture in my mind of what my future would look like. As my dream grew, the elephant slowly began to shrink. However, it did not disappear completely; it stubbornly clung to the inner fringes of my psyche, and it would take many years for considerable healing to take place in my heart.

In the meantime, continuous and deliberate learning spurred me on and out of the pit of desperation. This process pointed me towards opening myself up to help from other sources. I systematically identified the areas of leadership and growth that I needed to work on. I doggedly pursued the knowledge that was to help me improve on them.

Remember, admitting that you do not know something doesn't make you vulnerable. It strengthens you. You are able to learn from others who have struggled with the same issues and succeeded.

One thing I had not anticipated was how long it took me to deal with the elephant in the room. It finally came together well into my adult life when flying back home from a business trip. I had to embrace the principle of the gaping mouth. When travelling, I enjoy endless learning opportunities. Overnight flights are particularly stressful for me, as I hardly get any sleep. I am one of those folk who need to be completely horizontal and tucked into a warm cozy bed for any meaningful sleep to kick in. On this particular flight, after a long, restless night of trying to engage with the inflight entertainment, I needed to go to the restroom. It was 6:00 A.M.

As my seat was at the front of the economy class cabin, I had to walk down the isle to the back of the cabin to the restrooms. The ones up front were reserved for the first-class passengers, the guys in spacious seats who had paid top dollar for a ride in the same *tin can* I was in. An interesting sight greeted me: lo and behold, there lay a sea of gaping mouths in various degrees of relaxation. A smile crossed my lips and I had to stifle a chuckle that was threatening to spill out. These were the same people I had stood in line with at the boarding gates hours before, all looking very dignified as we waited to fly. Now, in the small hours of the morning, overtaken by sleep and fatigue, they looked much less refined. Some were even drooling slightly!

There, laid out in plain sight were three important lessons on leadership, lessons that would help me deal with any elephant that would try to creep into the same abode with me in the future.

The first lesson was that it is essential for a leader to trust other people, in addition to having faith in self. I needed to trust that there was good in the people close to me in my life, people who would be willing to help me and embrace my ideals. As I looked at the gaping mouths, there were endless possibilities for entertaining myself: I could have popped some salt into their mouths, or stuffed their noses with the black pepper that I hadn't used from my dinner tray. Trust was critical if I was to become a leader at home. I would have to grow my family into a trust-laden basket; full of belief in each other and the community we lived in. The bottom line is: with more trust bestowed upon them, family members will be empowered to live as a team, yet still be given space to grow individually.

The second lesson was that it was necessary for me to be willing to surrender more. I could not possibly hold the whole world in my hands. In other words, I needed to stop playing God. These passengers had completely submitted to a necessary natural process. During sleep, your body rebuilds and restores itself from the rigors of life. Sleep restores balance. My leadership is only as good as my willingness to work with my followers. There has to be an intricate balance between my family and myself. He who thinks he is a leader and has no followers is only taking a walk.

Lesson number three was that, as a leader, it was all right for me to show some vulnerability. I was not Superman, and no one expected me to be anyway. What made the elephant in my room larger than life was that I had become incessantly dependent on what other people thought or said about me. I was a prisoner to peer pressure, as I did not want my weaknesses exposed. Even as some of the passengers drooled, the most pressing issue to them was the need for rest. I could laugh at them, but the reality was that it was them laughing at me. Come morning, their drool would be washed off, but I would still be very sleepy and grumpy. I learned that it was okay to be vulnerable and accept my weaknesses—and that this was necessary if I was to become a strong, credible leader. I needed to stop trying to fit in when I was born to stand out.

The next step was to establish strong boundaries around me. It was time to keep the good in and the bad out.

Building Boundaries

Going back to my teenage years, I remember my dogged determination to live a life different from my Dad's. The path I set myself on even defied the general wisdom that insists common sense has been removed from even the most rational teenage mind.

During all national holidays, my grandfather's tradition was to slaughter a sheep and have his extended family over to celebrate. These were times of celebration, glorious moments that would sometimes bring four generations together under one roof. It was an opportunity to listen to fables from my great-grandmother, a time to run riot with my cousins and eat as much candy as my stomach could handle.

However, there was a dark side to these seemingly glorious times. An enemy prowled in the background, so subtle that no one seemed to notice. Well, not everyone was blind to this issue; one event when I was twelve has remained etched deep in my mind, as it completely changed the way I would think and engage with others from that time forward. The event was a major turning point in my life, a milestone that shaped my future. As I sat next to my favorite aunt, she invited me to take a few sips of an alcoholic drink she had in her hand. Even at this young age, I believed that drinking alcohol wasn't the right thing to do. I had seen its negative effects on my Dad and Granddad and did not want anything to do with it. As much as I did not even take a sip of her drink, I felt my innocence torn away from me. There was a deep feeling of fear and loss. It was evident that those who were supposed to protect my innocent mind seemed bent on ensuring my destruction.

To some extent, my mother, who was and still is a firm Christian, was instrumental in guiding me on the vices I needed to avoid. She had instilled in me the love of God and His ways, mainly through her fervent prayers. However, what she did not prepare me for was how to deal with these dangers when they crept up on me, masquerading as innocent parts of everyday life. In essence, I did not have the know-how to develop healthy boundaries against negative external influence. Maybe she was not aware of the pressure I faced, even from close family members.

It was only by the grace of God that I managed to navigate through those difficult periods.

Much later, in my mid-twenties, I encountered a life-changing piece of work that explained what I had developed (albeit unknowingly) to shelter myself. In their book, *Boundaries*, Doctors

Henry Cloud and John Townsend provided me with a very profound picture of what boundaries are. "Boundaries define us. They define what is me and what is not me. A boundary shows me where I end and someone else begins, leading me to a sense of ownership," they say.[6]

If only every human being would embrace this. The world would be totally different! Respect for boundaries would have prevented wars, bloodshed, one group of people being alienated from another... the list goes on. However, Cloud and Townsend go a little further to say that we should not consider boundaries as walls; rather, they are fences with gates in them so that the good can be allowed in, and the bad cast out.

Boundaries define who you are, what you do, who you relate with, and how you behave. In addition to cementing parental authority, setting boundaries in the home, and in my own life has been necessary. I had to use the big "3 R's": Rules, Routines, and Responsibilities.

In *Parent* Power, John Rosemond[7] expounds that "Together, [the "3 R's"] organize, stabilize, and energize my children's lives. They bring order to potential chaos. They give the child a sense of direction and purpose, and they are the framework in which life takes form and substance. Without them, the child is sure to flounder."

Rules have to guide how we interact with each other as a family and with the external world. They help us to understand what is permissible, what is negotiable and what is to be avoided at all costs. Rules help us to understand what is expected of us, how those expectations fit into big picture of our engagement, and the consequences of disobeying the rules. Rules bring order to potential chaos.

One thing we discovered early in our married life is that *routines* play a major role in our growth and interactions. Routines are sequences of actions that we regularly followed; they include morals, self-control, habits, etc. Routines are important in the training process and the rules help to reinforce them.

Responsibilities are what help growth with a sense of purpose. A purpose to develop oneself as well as benefit the community we exist in. Without grasping responsibility for our actions, we participate in active or passive disobedience. Responsibilities are a key component of the socialization process, where we learn to become better organized and work together to stabilize and energize the environment we live in.

After my wife and I got married, I desperately needed to establish healthy boundaries for my family to exist within. These boundaries may not have been able to protect them from external attacks and vulnerabilities; however, they would come in handy when they needed to sift through the fog of unfamiliar – and familiar – challenges that would drift their way from time to time. I was very fortunate to link up with a group that was exploring Cloud and Townsend's great book, *Boundaries,* wherein those two brilliant minds explore what they refer to as the "Ten Laws of Boundaries" that I adopted and later adapted for my life and family. These laws address what we need to do in order to grow our relationships with other people. I grouped the ten laws into two categories: emotional and physical boundaries.

Emotional boundaries (Laws 1-8) were the most challenging to deal with. They had to do with delving deep into my mind.

Physical boundaries (Laws 9 and 10) related to my interaction with anything external to me.

These "Ten Laws of Boundaries" by Dr. Cloud and Dr. Townsend are as follows:

First, the *Emotional Boundaries:*

[Law 1] The Law of Sowing and Reaping: It says that none of the actions we do will be without consequences. Cause and effect was

the first thing I had to deal with. I realized that if I was to lead from the home front, I had to fill my heart and mind with positive and edifying knowledge. I also had to practice what I said was good. For example, I can't expect my children to clean after themselves when I can't clear the mess I have caused in a room. The consequence is that I will have to spend time to clean up. My children have to see me practically applying the principle for the appropriate behavior to be instilled in their lives. This Law, say Cloud and Townsend, "...gives us reasonable sense of the power of control over our lives."

[Law 2] The Law of Responsibility: The next step is that I had to take control of the decisions or actions I made. This included taking charge of my feelings and how I reacted or responded to external stimuli. I am responsible for my feelings, only I could make myself contented. I had realized that some friends or work colleagues would make mistakes and expect me to resolve them on their behalf. However, when this persisted, I realized I was not only being irresponsible for the time I should have been spending on more constructive issues, I was abetting their inability to take ownership of their repeated mistakes.

[Law 3] The Law of Power: The power to do things that would help me overcome life's dangerous hurdles was in my hands. I had to believe in myself and have confidence that I could make it. The interesting feature of power is it sometimes gets into my head. I may think I am invincible, that I can do anything I want by sheer might. The reality is that I eventually find out that I am not all that powerful when I fail at some activity or chore. However, Cloud and Townsend remind me that I have power to agree with the truth about my problems, submit to my inability, seek for solutions, turn from evil, humble myself and ask for help, and make amends.

[Law 4] The Law of Respect: This reminds me that I am not the only one that matters. It taught me to be careful to judge others' boundaries, as mine may face similar judgment. I struggled with

how feasible it was for me to do this without compromising my faith or a promise I had committed to. But as I learned to respect other peoples' boundaries, I began to appreciate why others should respect mine too. I had to learn to love again in order to stand for the truth without fear. And with this came freedom and the ability to love openly. Love and respect go hand in hand.

[Law 5] The Law of Motivation: What keeps me doing the things that I do? Is it the out of love or the need to "fit" in (fear of rejection)? This law informs us of the false motives that restrict our boundary setting. Fear, guilt, anger, loneliness, seeking approval, are just some of the factors that holds us back. I had to work very hard to overcome all these negative motives that drove my behavior and limited my ability to lead mind. There is one phrase from Cloud and Townsend that liberated me: "Freedom first, service second. If you serve to get free of your fear, you are doomed to failure." I absolutely love that! Many times I had to dig into the depths of myself to find some motivation. However, I gradually built a support system around me to keep grounded.

[Law 6] The Law of Evaluation: Where am I? Do the relationships I have matter? Are there mistakes, issues, and habits I need to let go? Are my actions or inactions entrenching mediocrity? One Saturday afternoon, I went through my cellphone address book. It was amazing how many contacts had not been used in months! I slowly and deliberately deleted them, and as I did, my load grew lighter. I no longer needed to hide behind the number of people I knew; instead, I could focus on the relationships that truly mattered.

[Law 7] The Law of Proactivity: All forces exists in pairs, the actions and reaction are simultaneous. Without a safety valve, the forces generated within a pressure cooker may elevate to such levels as to result in a massive explosion. Like a pressure cooker, I realized how important it was for me to carefully design a safety valve—something put in place specifically in anticipation of

possible problems, designed to stop those problems before they cause irreparable damage. I began setting proactive boundaries. "Proactive people show what they love, what they want, what they purpose, and what they stand for." note Cloud and Townsend.

[Law 8] The Law of Envy: I found out that I was progressively making decisions based on the need to fit in with the crowd. "Keeping up with the Joneses" was dominating my life by trying to get what others had just because it looked good. It was time to live life at my pace. I had to remain steadfastly focused on my Family Vision.

Finally, the *Physical Boundaries:*

[Law 9] The Law of Activity: To me, this means always striving to do my best regardless of the circumstances. As I discovered how to live my life with my Family Vision as a guide, I had to become like a child again; in a sense, it was like re-learning how to walk, talk, and write. Whereas before I had simply drifted along, *reacting* to my circumstances, now every activity I undertook was purpose-driven.

[Law 10] The Law of Exposure: I did not exist in a perfect world. I needed to build healthy relationships; however, I also needed to have an effect on those relationships. On a regular basis, I made the effort to clearly identify my boundaries and communicate them so that others knew what they were and where they had been set.

When advising actor Sidney Poitier on the balance between life and his acting career, director John Cassavetes said this, "Let me tell you something… We are good friends, but never, ever do an artistic favor for a friend. Loan friends money, be there for them in any other way, but don't do them any artistic favors, because you've got to have one area of your life where there's no room for compromise." What strong imagery to drive home the need for boundaries! Each of us must choose for ourselves those areas in our lives where we will not compromise.

For me, the area of no compromise is my family. This provides me with the perfect opportunity to practice having integrity, loving fully, failing forwards (learning without fear), showing mercy, and growing exponentially. This well-defined zone is the one facet in life that provides refuge for my children and wife.

What Is Your Name?

I recently came across a very interesting but sad description of a family's lineage. Dr. Kevin Leman[8] describes his as 'A Well-Watered Ancestry'. This is not to be confused with the charming, progressive, and healthy type of ancestry. "I come from a long line of drinkers," says Dr. Leman. "Virtually all Lemans enjoyed slugging down a few cold ones. Okay, not a few. *Many.*" Not many people I know desire to provide such an ancestry, or leave a similar foundation for their family.

When we first discovered that we were going to become parents, my wife and I had very different reactions. To be certain and remove any shadow of doubt that our first baby was on the way, we opted to perform the more reliable blood test. We waited anxiously as the technician worked his magic in his laboratory deep within the maze of the medical facility. Suspense lay thick in the air. We had looked forward to this pregnancy. Our prayers had been fervent, as we both so dearly loved children.

Then the results were presented to us on a tiny printed piece of paper. My wife was pregnant! It is difficult to describe the joy I felt, my heart nearly burst with pride. I was going to be a father! I wanted to jump up onto the chairs in the lobby and shout out loud, "I'm going to be a daddy! Yeah!" My wife on the other hand was very calm. Apart from a hint glaze in her eyes, she looked very composed. The results were a confirmation of her intuition of the tiny precious life that was growing in her.

The most amazing transformation happened as soon as we stepped out of the clinic. My wife says that it seemed like I went into a trance. I did not speak to her all the way home. She was very concerned, worried that I may have been putting up a front about wanting to have children. What she didn't know was that I was going through a harrowing discussion with myself. The pregnancy test was just a confirmation that I needed to step up and start thinking like a father... a father I had no clue how to become.

Questions ravaged my poor mind like a bad storm, tearing at my insides like the worst tornado ever. Would I be a good father? How would I take care of my growing family? What if I lost my job, then what? Will the baby steal the time I had to spend with my wife? Would my employer insist on sending me out on trips for extended periods? These, and so many more unanswerable questions piled up.

In essence, my mind was desperately trying to answer one critical question. It was trying to call out, "What is your name?" It was a desperate attempt to begin molding my definition of family and the identity that would anchor my life, and those of my wife and coming child. After a few agonizing hours, my wife finally got through to me. You should have seen the relief on my wife's face when she realized that my silence was only a measure of my excitement, and my determination to do right by my growing family.

The next port of call was to start thinking about the name that our child would be known by. A name! We searched everywhere; we agonized day and night. To complicate matters further, we would hear nothing about any pre-screening to find out whether it was a boy or a girl. Finally, we came up with a solution: we would find a name that was unisex.

There was going to be one major trajectory away from the norm: our children would not be named after anybody else in our families. Why not? Tradition held that anyone in his or her right mind would make sure that the family name was perpetuated. In our culture, children are named after their grandparents. For example, since I am the first-born boy, I was named after my paternal grandfather. My brother was named after my maternal grandfather. In essence, I am my grandfather's *reincarnation*, and he refers to me as his age-mate. Yet here my wife and I were, furiously hacking at our respective family trees with every conceivable tool we could lay our hands on. It looked senseless, or so other people thought. However, there was a lot of symbolism in this seemingly mad deviation from common norms.

To appreciate where my wife and I were coming from, we will have to go back to the beginning. As I mentioned, mine was a dysfunctional family. I too had a *well-watered* ancestry, especially on my father's side. My grandfather loved alcohol. I have no recollection of a single night he came home sober during those days we would be visiting him and my grandmother. My uncle and two aunties also partied hard. Alcohol was a central feature in any family event—it is a miracle that some of us did not end up thoroughly drunk at a very tender age!

With this background, it is not surprising that I had to break traditions that were not healthy for my life, or that of my new family. It was time to reclaim the dignity of the *name*. The identity I would bestow upon my child would go against common-speak and stand out for its resilience, integrity, and above all, a spirit of servant-leadership.

Naming our children was not going to be routine, it was not simply a labeling process. It was a re-birth for my wife and I. We were going to bestow a legacy upon our children. From birth they were going to walk in the promise, a promise that they were made for greatness. (Please note that by "in greatness" I do not necessarily mean they will become celebrities or some beings with an elevated social status. I would not mind if they do, but this is not to be the primary focus of their lives). My mind recalled a verse of scripture, Genesis 32:28. Speaking to the son of Isaac after many trials, God says, "Your name will no longer be Jacob, but Israel, because you have struggled with God and with humans and have overcome." The naming process here was not just symbolic, it was like a re-birth and the beginning of a new dispensation of hope and growth.

In a similar fashion, the names I would give my children were just the first step to a future where they would become people that matter. Their names would inspire hope and provide a legacy for our family. As my wife and I first met in southern Africa, we thought it was important for us to give our children names from that part of the world. It would be the beginning of a new legacy, one of hope.

Our first child, a girl, we named *Tinashe* that means, "God is with us." Our second child, a boy, would always remind us of our gratitude to God for our family. So we called him *Tatenda*, "We thank you." Finally, we were blessed with another girl whom we named *Tumelo*. Her name means "faith" and reminds us of our faith in God.

Do Not Excuse Misdemeanor

Picture this: your bedroom window has a few broken panes. Wind and rain buffet you all night and you can find no comfort in your sleep. The following day, on your way from work, you pass by the store and stock up on blankets, a ski mask, weatherproof jacket and pants, and a pair of swimming goggles to boot. After a sumptuous dinner—you do need the calories, of course, as another cold night looms—you don your gear confident of a warm night and good sleep.

Does this sound ridiculous? Of course it does!

What sensible people do is to call the glazier and have the broken window fixed. They do not give excuses of why the wind and rain are pouring in. They do not work around the problem, they nip it in the bud. In doing so, they protect themselves from further harm or damage.

Does the example above resonate with you? Are you the parent that lets your child get off the hook when they misbehave? To add salt to injury, do you even go to the extent of providing lengthy and detailed excuses for what the child has done? In reality, what you are doing is perpetuating misbehavior in the child. "She must be sleepy"; "He is such a sensitive boy"; "Peas are just not her thing"; "It must be the new environment that he does not like"… the excuses pile on thick and fast.

Adults are as capable of wrongdoing as any child is. The difference is that we as the parent have a full understanding of right and wrong, and in choosing the wrong we may be compounding the sin by rejecting the opportunity to provide leadership in certain situations. By doing so—by our own failure to lead—we set up our children to fail, both now and in the future when they have become the adults.

Consider *Mother Fries*, a real-life mum to a French-fry-crazy three-year-old boy. She had a busy job that was wearing her down. By the time she got home, all she wanted to do was collapse on the couch and sleep till morning. But her growing son needed his dinner. However, when the food hit the table he mutated into a shrieking freak! He threw tantrums to avoid eating his healthy meal. Why? Because all he wanted to eat was fries. He would wail and scream until his mother succumbed to his unhealthy desire.

The fat-laden fries were an assured highway to his destiny with obesity and poor health. Instead of taking command of the situation and dealing directly with the misconduct, the mother excused his behavior by saying, "He needs to eat. As a growing boy, I cannot just watch him go to bed hungry."

The shocker was when she overheard conversation between her boy and his neighborhood buddy. "When you want something, just scream and cry loud and long enough," said her son. "After some time, your mummy will give in and give it to you. That is what I do when I want to eat fries." She was gob smacked! It was not long before fries were totally exterminated from the household menu.

Fortunately, this mum was quick enough to fix her broken window before the wind and storms drove into her house.

"The WISE man builds his house on the ROCK instead of sinking sand; for when the storms of life descend, that house will surely stand." Sper. What leadership are you providing for your child's foundation? Is it rock solid, or exclusively sandy?

3. Courage to Change

"Courage is the most important of all virtues, because without courage you can't practice any other virtue consistently. You can practice any virtue erratically, but nothing consistently without courage."
—*Maya Angelou*

Responsible |adjective| • having an obligation to do something, or having control over or care for someone

Leaders Must Be Responsible

As a leader, I am fully responsible to myself first, and then to those whom I am entrusted with the opportunity to lead. I can only give what I have. It is therefore paramount that I invest in knowledge that will help increase my character and leadership skills. Only then will I even begin to claim the right to lead my family and others. Please note the sequential progression here: before I can legitimately lead others genuinely from the heart, I first have to make sure that my home is in order.

Leadership is more about empowering others and providing validation of another than being in a position of authority. In doing this, I provide the inspiration or *push* to help someone else achieve a goal that they were unsure they could attain. Benjamin Disraeli once said, "The greatest good you can do for another is not just to share your riches but to him his own." If my desire to lead is for my own glorification, this just shoots me down from my lofty ideals. Leadership is not about *me* as it is all about *others*.

In pursuit of knowledge, I do not strive to get more education as we have come to embrace it in the form of certificates and titles. I will not spend thousands of dollars trying to get more degrees than a thermometer! That will only prepare me for a profession. To become an effective leader, I choose to seek out the wisdom and knowledge of other leaders that will teach me the life-lessons needed for success. To lead, I must become teachable. I have to become vulnerable to become teachable. To do this I must find a credible mentor to whom I am fully accountable for all my actions – successes, failures, and anything else in between.

Otto von Bismarck believed that "A fool learns from experience. A wise man learns from the experience of others." The moment you stop learning, you hang up your gloves on leadership. A leader is forever thirsty for knowledge, restless with the status quo, and always challenging themselves to become better at what they do.

Back when I began my journey to raise my family according to my Vision, it was not a difficult choice for me to accept that I need to be more responsible for the focus of my development as a leader. In essence, I had to embrace my fear of failure at becoming a leader. This was the only way I could get the power over my life back to myself.

Change Hurts

Making the first move was the most challenging prospect I could contemplate. This daunting move was comprised of taking a hard look at hurtful things to which I had turned a blind eye. I had been hiding behind the falsehood that, given enough time, difficult issues will eventually resolve on their own accord, like a fire that eventually burns out after the fuel is exhausted.

When our first-born was two years old, she loved playing hide-and-seek; well… any two-year-old anywhere in the world loves to play hide-and-seek. She would pretend to count as I scurried away to find a foxhole to hide in. Her joy was in me jumping out of my hiding place with a roar. She would then waddle away in a fit of delightful squeals. The hilarious part of this game was when the tables were turned. When it was her time to hide, instead of running off to find a suitable hiding place, where Daddy could not find her, she simply covered her eyes. At first, this puzzled me. Why wasn't she hiding? Then it dawned on me that, to her perception, as long as she could not see me, the converse was also true: I could not see her. She was in the best hiding place… her mind!

This analogy comes to life in us when we are forced to change the way we think, act, and relate with others. When confronted with the need to change, do you find the prospect an adventure? Does it offer you the opportunity to become creative in finding the best foxholes to explore? Or is it time for you to hide and assume that the issue will somehow resolve itself?

When I was growing up, my father was hardly ever at home. This affected me both physically and emotionally. I needed my childhood hero to walk me through the maze that is life. But he was not there. When I grew up, I had two choices: live my Dad's evidently broken model or develop one of my own. I chose to go my own way.

I chose to chart out my own path to my desired goals. This was the most significant and painful change I was to endure. It forced me to wade through minefields of uncertainty as I tried to find my identity. I envied my friends who seemed to have great relationships with their fathers. Anxiety and self-consciousness tore at my heart and mind. Would I be able to pull it off? Like my daughter, I could cover my eyes and pretend that all was well—in essence, that's what I had been doing for so long. However, to move forward, I chose to embrace the change that would relieve me of the shackles of my past.

"When you are up to your rear end in alligators, it's hard to remember that your purpose is draining the swamp," George Napper reminds us. With no point of reference in sight, I had to rely on the Vision that I had developed when I was a gangly twelve-year-old. I had to remind myself that draining the swamp (the Vision) was the focus in order to kill the alligators (my Dad's broken model) had to be slayed. I had to consciously choose to be present for my family when the time came. There is still much more to talk about with regards to change and responsibility, but I will explore my role in my family in more detail in Chapter 4: Presence Rocks!

Tackle Mediocrity

I soon discovered the cancer that was impeding my ability to embrace change. For a long time, mediocrity had had a death grip on my heart. It did not help that I constantly received negative comments from my uncles and aunties. And my father, who should have been building me up, offered no significant advice one way or the other, neither mentoring nor helping me with the ropes of life. He was virtually, and literally, absent. My poor mother tried all she could to help me, but how was she to know what to do with a fiercely independent-minded, testosterone-driven teenager? By the time I was fourteen years old, I was rapidly approaching 6 feet of height, practically towering over her five-foot-five frame.

Mediocrity permeated throughout my whole extended family. There was a common trait: just do what was necessary to get by. To my father's credit, he tried to place us in good schools, but this hurt more than it helped. Mingling with other kids from well-off backgrounds was savagely brutal. For example, I could not afford to buy a hot meal for lunch. As other kids made a beeline for the cafeteria, or sunk their teeth into meaty sandwiches, I had to be content with some cold meal when even that much was available. It was heart wrenching, but that was all my mother could afford. I have a lot of admiration for my mother for her creativity with what little food she had at her disposal. Such small quantities, and to top it all off, most of the time, the variety was limited to a maximum of three food items at any one time. My mother ensured that we were as comfortable as she possibly could. To this day, I still do not have a clue how she managed to do that. I still draw a lot of inspiration from her deep wells of strength, resolve, and resourcefulness.

Why was mediocrity so rife in my family? I mulled over this for years on end. Then I began a critical analysis of my grandfathers. When I was young, never at any time when I was visiting with them did I hear them talk of their children. There were never any stories of how my parents and their siblings grew up, no narrative of family conquests, challenges, or failures… Nothing! All that was discussed were the politics of the day, whose daughter was getting married, a distant relative who had passed on. It was as if discussing family issues was taboo.

Later on, when I was much older, it dawned on me that my grandfather was hardly at home during my father's formative years. Perhaps, my father was acting out the only thing he knew: just get by, provide the bare minimum, send out a wishful prayer, and hope for the best.

Growing up, was life made too easy for my relatives? Did their parents help them towards mediocrity? Were they introduced to a work ethic? How about morals? What had they leaned from any adversity they faced?

I may not fully understand the circumstances my relatives grew up in, but I believe that the answers to these questions had a lot had to do with how their parents' behaved.

My paternal grandfather was a very influential man in his day. At on time, he was the mayor of our town. He had the ear of the elite in business and politics. He could have amounted to anything he wanted to become. Where I come from, he who owns land is king. My grandfather owned plots of prime land. But what did he choose to do with that real estate? He sold it off and squandered all the money on alcohol and women.

One incident will remain burned into my memory forever. While walking on the streets of the town I grew up in, I overheard a conversation that confirmed some utterances my paternal grandfather would occasionally make while drunk. Two women were discussing their escapades with him. They had no idea who I was, and therefore, the discussion was quite descriptive in its detail. To say the least, I was not very proud to carry my family name at that point in time. How I wished the earth would open up and swallow me whole!

Can you start to see a pattern emerging here? I did. It was a classic case of a generational curse at play. I did not like the pattern I saw, so I made a choice to change it. I chose leadership over the curse. With a vision and a plan, and the help of God, I would bring the cycle to a screeching halt.

Chapter 14, verse 18 of Numbers says, "The LORD is slow to anger, abounding in love and forgiving sin and rebellion. Yet he does not leave the guilty unpunished; he punishes the children for the sin of the parents to the third and fourth generation."[9]

Now, that was a very scary proposition to me, something akin to the preview of a horror movie script! Considering the character of my father and grandfather, this passage took on heavy gravity for me. This is not what I had envisioned for my own family. I took a hard look at myself and determined in my heart that change was needed. It was going to take a lot of hard work, but I prayed for wisdom, and for the strength to live God's will. My prayer was answered in the following passage from Ezekiel Chapter 18, verses 19 and 20.[10]

"Yet you ask, 'why does the son not share the guilt of his father?' Since the son has done what is just and right and has been careful to keep all my decrees, he will surely live. The one who sins is the one who will die. The child will not share the guilt of the parent, nor will the parent share the guilt of the child. The righteousness of the righteous will be credited to them, and the wickedness of the wicked will be charged against them."

Consider this: The inconvenient truth is that many of us are spending long hours at work at the expense of spending enough time to lead our children. Every day, we must evaluate, asking ourselves if this is the case with our own life. To be a leader at home, I need to *be at* home. And then as a leader at home, I need to expose my children to learning opportunities: explore new worlds, make correct decisions, and grow in wisdom. This is not a comfortable place to be. We may need to reduce the time we spend away from home.

It is amazing what power water has. When it is held back behind a dam and forced to exit through pipes or tunnels, water can turn huge turbines to generate electricity. When heated to boiling temperature, water produces steam. At 211 degrees Fahrenheit, water is merely hot. At 212 degrees, it boils. With boiling water comes steam that can power a locomotive or a turn a huge turbine to produce electricity. That one extra degree makes all the difference.

I was fortunate to have a loving and caring Mum. As much as she was struggling to bring up a teenager nearly by herself, she provided a starting point for me. She was that extra degree that spurred me on to become a better leader.

Growing up with my family was like playing on a team that was entrenched in total mediocrity. My pre-programing seemed to have predisposed me to abhor any form of responsibility. Like a soccer club that has realized it will never win a championship with its current roster, it was time to rethink my history, training, and team-building processes. I needed to understand where each team member was coming from—and where he or she were headed—to understand if they had any potential help me excel in the future. I found our that many of my relatives did not care much for taking responsibility of their actions, nor did they really care about the consequences of their inaction.

From this starting point, I began the process of identifying a system that would inspire my new team—my wife and three children. I knew my leadership would have to be personal, present, and deliberate. I had to become their mentor, teacher, and companion as they traversed through life. I couldn't stand on the sidelines; I had to be in the game. And I couldn't give 99 percent; it had to be 100 percent. That extra effort could change everything. Just as with boiling water, time repeatedly proved that the single degree that makes all the difference. For my wife and children, that extra effort I put in would determine how they perceived and interacted with life in general.

Seek Inspiration... Voraciously!

Growing up, my family knew more lean times than days of plenty. Sometimes there would be so little to go around that I would go without lunch at school. Now, let me clarify that there are people who have been in more dire situations than I was. But back then I would watch my classmates munching away at hot dogs, sandwiches, and cake while I consumed copious amounts of *air-burgers*. This was tough to deal with, both mentally and emotionally.

Having nothing else to turn to, I devised a method to add *salt and pepper* to my meals. I did not want to bother my poor mother. She cared (and still cares) very much about all her children. Voicing my thoughts about the food would only have propelled her blood pressure off the charts. So instead of bothering her, I chose a very interesting method to block out the torment I was going through: books became my solace. When the food was unpalatable, sometimes nothing more than a plate of potatoes and mealy meal, I choose to read through it.

As we could not even afford to buy one storybook, I had acquired a dog-eared copy of *Famous Five* by Enid Blyton from a friend in school. In the book were scenes of a table decked with fried eggs, bacon, freshly baked bread, and fruit. It may sound trivial, but when the only thing on my table was a bowl of plain porridge, the book was a heavenly distraction. The stomach can handle anything the mind instructs it to; I am living proof of that!

In his memoir, *The Measure of a Man*, Sidney Poitier,[11] the first African-American to win the Academy Award for best actor, vividly describes what self-inspiration can yield, if you only have the courage and discipline to pursue it.

"The page of want-ad boxes faced the theatrical page, on which sat an article with a heading that read ACTORS WANTED. The gist of the article was that there was a group called the American Negro Theatre was in need of actors for its next production. My mind got spinning. My eyes bounced back and forth between the want-ad page and the theatrical page…

"But when I went in and was auditioned on the spot, the man in charge quickly let me know – in no uncertain terms – that I was misguided in my assumptions. I had no training in acting. I could barely read! And to top it off, I had a thick, singsong Bahamian accent.

"He snatched the script from my hands, spun me around, grabbed me by the scruff of my neck and the back of my pants, and marched me on my tippy toes toward the door. He was seething. 'You just get out of here and stop wasting people's time. Go get a job you can handle,' he barked. And just as he threw me out, he ended with, 'Get yourself a job as a dish-washer or something.'

"I have to tell you his comments stung worse than any wasp on any sapodilla tree back in my childhood. His assessment was like a death sentence for my soul. I had never mentioned to him that I was a dishwasher. How did he know? If he did not know, what was it all about me that implied to this stranger that dishwashing would accurately sum up my whole life's worth?

"Whatever it was, I knew I had to change it, or life was going to be mighty grim… So I set out on a course of self-development. I worked nights and on my meal-breaks…sat near the entrance to the kitchen, reading newspapers, trying to sound out each syllable of each unfamiliar word."

Poitier went on to flunk out again, but he was resilient. He worked out a deal where he became the theatre's janitor. He became an understudy while sweeping the walk and stoking the wood stove. To cut the long story short, he eventually made the cut and finally made on to the stage. It was not easy, but his persistence and self-motivation paid off. He used a negative experience as inspiration to work and learn, and change his life.

This script was very similar to that of my life. I have worked hard to launch myself from a platform of negativity into a future of hope and positive experiences. The only difference is that I have not made it to Hollywood yet!

Man, Love Their Mum

Let us face it men, we drew the short stick as far as our children are concerned. Our precious women have a wild head start on us. For nine months, or thereabouts, our children have the opportunity to bond with their mothers.

During the time my wife carried our babies, I was just some distant rumble that interrupted their communion with Momma. They consistently heard Momma's voice, even when she was sleep-talking. Her heartbeat was their cue that they would live, as long as Momma was alive. The rumble of her stomach as her digestive juices processed their meal brought peace to them; it meant that they would not starve to an early death. As her lungs filled to capacity with fresh oxygen, it meant that their little hearts could breath life to their new muscles. To a baby, Momma is life.

In his book *Wild at Heart: Discovering the Secret of a Man's Soul*[12] John Eldredge provides us with a powerful description of who Mum is. Not only does she provide nurture but she is also the aide-de-camp. "Eve is given to Adam as his *ezer kenegdo* – or as many translations have it, his 'help meet' or 'helper.'…But Robert Alter says this is a 'notoriously difficult word to translate'. It means something far more powerful than just 'helper'; it means '*lifesaver.*' The phrase is only used elsewhere of God, when you need him to come through for you desperately. 'There is no one like the God of *Jeshurun*, who rides on the heavens to help you' (Deut. 33:26).

"Eve is the life giver; she is Adam's ally. It is to both of them that the charter for adventure is given. It will take both of them to sustain life. And they both need to fight together." *[sic]*

It is, therefore, a state-of-emergency when your children see or have any notion that you do not love their mum any more. I remember wondering in my youth what kind of human being would hate my Mum so much as to abandon her. Many nights I pondered what had become of my father. Why did he not care for my dear mother anymore? Why was he silent to her pleas for help at home in bringing up their four (eventually five) children? I could not comprehend, and this was frustrating. As I tried to process these thoughts, the more the distance between my father and I became. In my estimation, he evolved into this heartless beast that was to be avoided at all cost.

My dear brothers, loving your wife is critical in bringing leadership back home. Without absolute love, you cannot expect to draw any respect from your children, your wife's feelings not withstanding.

Some men have this misplaced fallacy that to love is easy. An occasional box of chocolate, a bouquet of flowers, and a beautiful house on the hill... These things may work, but only for a season. Then the rubber hits the road and life gets real. Work is required, commitment and dedication, not platitudes and presents. You see, when we were called to love, it is unconditional, no pre-nuptial agreements or escape scenarios.

As life would have it, we may not always agree on all matters in the home. Periods of tension will arise from time to time. A few years back, our mentor couple shared with us an interesting story. One day, they could not come to an agreement on an issue. This precipitated silence between the two of them. That evening, as they settled at the table for dinner, their only child, who was about two years old, sat between them. As they bowed their heads to say grace, as was their custom before any meal, two little hands swung to action. Grabbing each of his parent's lapels, he pulled their faces towards each other and, with a stern voice, instructed them to "Kiss!"

This two-year-old recognized strife and had the foresight to help resolve it, understanding that peace in the heart was essential if they were to continue their communion as a family. Young as he was, he had the innate knowledge that as long as love flourished, then his family would be okay.

Dads, love your children's mum. Do not lie to yourself that the kids will not notice. They do, and will one day hold you to account for your misdeeds.

Says Michael Hyatt, one of the great men who most inspire me, "The most important gift you can give your children is to love their mother. How true—especially in an age when broken homes are increasingly the norm. A healthy marriage is a legacy that will pay dividends to your children and grandchildren for generations."[13]

Woman, Honor Their Dad

My precious wife agreed to step in here to offer her perspective on what honoring a Dad means. She also grew up learning how to do this from her own mum. Here is her story….

They were sprawled out on the kitchen floor shelling groundnuts from their pods when our seven-year-old daughter asked my wife this question: "Mama, where is Daddy from?" After some thought, my wife responded, "I don't know."

Our daughter also enquired after my wife's origins, punctuating her question with, "Please do not tell me that cradle-of-mankind-end-of-the-world mumbo jumbo!" This was easy. It took my dear wife a few minutes to tell our daughter about herself. It was, on the large part, a rosy account that left out her occasional spells of selfishness and conceitedness as a girl. Her parents can shine a floodlight on these tendencies at the drop of a hat, but there was no need for my wife to share these small fallacies with our daughter at that time. She shared with our daughter what a pleasant little girl she had been. My wife added that she cared deeply about those around her and took great care not to hurt anyone's feelings. What our daughter received was a glimpse into an amazing description of the perfect person that my wife is.

As their thumbs became progressively sore from the effects of the rough groundnut shells, so their tummies rumbled from the raw nuts they occasionally popped into their mouths. "Mama," our daughter persisted with a quizzical look on her face, "Is my daddy from another world?" My wife could not comprehend where our daughter was going with this. "There is only one Earth, but there are many corners in it, you know," was my wife's response to her. She might have hinted that this handsome man was indeed from another world! According to my wife, I sometimes come across as an alien on weed. Apparently, at these moments I look like a lunatic cruising through a battlefield with no comprehension of its inherent dangers. My urgency to accomplish certain tasks can raise the hairs on her neck to their very ends and leave her teeth on edge! My intensity is enviable to the point of leaving my dear wife walking high on stilts in complete admiration of my focus.

Without much ado, she blurted, "Mama, I love you the way Daddy loves you!" Our daughter is like an insect with super-sensitive feelers. Just like her father, she believes the truth must be shared at all times, whether it gets you into trouble or not. I may occasionally be withdrawn and my wife can't seem to get through to me, periods thinks I transform into is a complete paradox! Yet she still loves me dearly and works at honoring me intently so my daughters can learn to honor whomever they marry in future. The legacy of honor and respect must start with her, right here at home, honoring this man from another world.

Our children's sense of security is anchored in the strength of the relationship between my wife and I. When my wife openly respects and honors their father, my children also find it easy to respect her as an authority in their lives.

As a daughter, wife, mother, friend, my wife cannot organize her affairs until she opens up her life to become subordinate to her Maker. My wife is His daughter first, then my wife. God would seem to say, "Precious child, love that seemingly self-seeking, arrogant man that makes your heart skip. Love him deeply, honor him all round, submit to his leadership, and let Me deal with him as his Master."

To love me can be very challenging, my wife thinks. Why will I not read her mind, be sensitive through all seasons, and talk to her at all times? These conflicts ravage her mind and sometimes manifest themselves outwardly in unpleasant ways. She can become irritable and non-responsive, and sometimes I have to retreat to the safety of our backyard to find some peace. Our children may sometimes tiptoe around her, unsure of their mother's mercurial mood.

My wife is the heart of our home. With her tender love and care, she provides nurture for all of us. Not that I do not do the same, it is only that she is a champion at it. Therefore, her tone can determine how a day pans out. With this in mind, she carefully works on sowing seeds of encouragement, spreading joy, and mending broken relationships. On the contrary, I am more results-oriented. "Just get it done!" I will tell my children on those occasions when I am impatient and feeling tired from the travails of life.

She still thinks I am from another planet, which might be true to some extent. However, she is willing to learn how things are done there. The simple fact that she wants to visit with this Martian is awesome! It drives me to open up to her more. It helps me to understand why I need to be gentler with my children, a pleasure I did not have with my own father.

"Mama, you were glowing," chimed our daughter as they finish shelling the last of the groundnuts. My wife wears her love for me on her sleeve. Our daughter's security is hinged on how she sees her treat me. Any negative utterance towards me sets the day's tone. Our daughter will be grumpy with those around her and non-responsive to simple instructions. She becomes difficult and will not eat her food. This calls on my wife to demonstrate respect and show what true service is. Martin Luther once said, "Let the wife make the husband glad to come home, and let him make her sorry to see him leave".

Bulletproof Your Heart and Mind

Considering that my wife and I have very different personalities, it is critical that we work very hard at understanding each other's temperaments. It all starts by me loving her and she honoring me. During this process, we both begin to understand our strengths and challenges in our relationship to each other. As in any relationship, there are times we go through challenges that may make or break that co-existence. If not handled well, the situation may end with one party withdrawing completely and seeking solace in an activity that violates the sanctity of the relationship.

That violation could be overindulging in alcohol, over-concentrating on a hobby, having an extra-marital affair, or spending excessive time with friends and work and away from our loved ones. The list can be endless. All these are what I consider affairs.

Affairs completely ruin the dynamics of your relationships. They are dangerous and like a deadly virus that slowly corrodes the very fabric of your life with your wife, or husband, as well as your children. In many cases, the damage is irreparable. Think of all the virtues you would like your family to embrace. Respectful, ethical, honest, virtuous, admirable, accountable, trustworthy… Well, just be involved in one affair and all these virtues nose-dive into a fiery oblivion!

All through my teens, I had a nagging feeling that my father was not completely honest with us. When he came home once every two months or so, he would spend much of his time with his friends. We would only see him early in the morning and late in the night. I had long suspected that my father was having an affair or two, but my feelings were nothing more than a hunch. However, these suspicions persistently gnawed at my conscience. After a long struggle with this issue, it became vividly clear to me that I needed peace in my heart and mind.

There was one major hitch, however: I did not have the dimmest clue where my father lived. We knew the town, but that was it. Thankfully, God would provide a valuable opportunity that finally led me to my father. It so happened that a close family friend who was concerned with our plight went to work in a town about 40 kilometers (25 miles) from where my father was stationed. Owing to his seniority at his workplace, our friend was able to track down the place where my father was living.

Plans were made for my father and I to meet. In my culture, the first-born male child becomes the de-facto leader at home in the absence of his father. I therefore hoped to take this challenge in stride, as was expected of me. What everyone did not see was the trepidation and turmoil I had boiling inside me. I was scared! How would my father react when we met?

I still remember that fateful day when I knocked at his door. You could have cut through the tension with a knife. My adrenaline level was off the charts and my heart was pounding so hard I thought it would burst out of my chest at any moment. It was as if I was about to get onto a battlefield! A soft, unsure tap at the door yielded no response. My second attempt was more successful; the door squeaked open and my worst fears were confirmed. Standing in the doorway was a woman, clearly not my mother. This was a woman that neither my mother nor my siblings knew of. Only my father...

and now me. What a terrible burden for a son to bear! Suddenly, life did not have meaning anymore. This was the end, or so I thought.

All I remember of that meeting was my father hugging me (for the first time in my life) and shedding tears, tears I did not believe were genuine or remorseful. I think he could not fathom that he had been caught with his hand in the cookie jar. The very core of my being was on fire! To this day, I still do not have a clue what her name was, nor do I remember what she looked like. Immediately, I detested my father; my enmity for him was indescribable! On that day he ceased to be my dad any more. Something in me died, and all I could think of him was as someone who donated some of the DNA that resides in my cells. He became just another hopeless man in a sea of many faces. As far as I was concerned, he had died.

After a few awkward moments, I went back to my friend's car and we drove off. That incident was never shared with my mother. I have never recounted the experience in any form until now, nearly twenty years later. I did not want anything to do with my father anymore. The thought that I carried his name and genes just left me very resentful of him. This bitterness nearly destroyed my life; I believe it would have if not for the faith in God that gave me hope.

Conventional wisdom has hoodwinked us into believing that affairs can only be sexual in nature. However, I eventually came to the realization that I could easily get stuck working long hours in order to provide my family with the trappings of modern life. It could be that I was trying to blot out some painful memories from my past. I could easily use this as an excuse for the selfish pursuit of the higher rungs of the corporate ladder, my quest to be considered by others as a successful man. My *affair* could easily be taking up long golfing weekends to help me build my business network. It could be heading to the bar to hook up with my mates, rather than going home to play with my children. It could be any of the myriad distractions and temptations that can pull even the most well meaning away from family.

Our lives have become deceptively unrealistic, and so steeped in misplaced priorities that we may sacrifice our families at the altar of future security. Then we discover it was naught but an illusion, a mirage—as soon as we get to it, it vanishes only to reappear away on the horizon. We must admit to ourselves that all these dreams we chase, payoffs that will never come, are affairs that we engage in. They rob our families of presence, dedication, and loyalty.

We must also recognize that, rather than physical, an affair may be emotional. These ties to those who are not our spouse are sometimes hidden deep in our hearts and minds. We may not even realize what we are doing until we take a long, hard, honest look at ourselves. But how do we start dealing with them? By making a conscious choice not only to be physically present, but also emotionally and spiritually too. "Nothing worth having comes without some kind of fight,"[14] Bruce Cockburn reminds us. It is time for me to fight for my family, starting with my intentional presence.

Irene Becker, in a comment to one of my blog posts, *One-degree Past Mediocrity,* said the following.

"I once wrote about how 'satisficing' is no longer enough. Satisficing is actually a word in the dictionary that describes mediocrity.

Although, I am optimistic and forward thinking, both come from being saddened by the mediocrity that surrounds us at every level of our lives and organizations. Part of this can be ascribed to what parent's model for children, but I would add that we have entire cultures that are mired in mediocrity, entire cultures that speak to the fact that we simply want to survive and get by. We do what we must, but do we need or want to do more?

I believe that the ability transcending mediocrity hinges on three things: empowerment, engagement and purpose. Parent should be empowering the best in their children, helping them develop an engagement and sense of purpose that takes them forward and helps them strive for excellence in everything they do. However, the best of parents can have children who have a predisposition towards mediocrity or whose peer group for an extended period of time influence and sway them.

Excellence starts in our heart, in our ability to know that trying to do our very best at any given moment is excellence in action. Our best may not suffice, but it will take us to a whole new level of growth and understand that pushes us forward.

Excellence can only be a fulcrum for human passion and potential when parents, educators, employers-when those in positions of authority remain resolute in creating communities of learning, sharing, caring-communities of engagement, empowerment and excellence where *purpose* and our ability to be our best and use our failures to fail forward is embraced and applauded.

The opportunity to create families, communities, and organizations of excellence is before us. May those who lead and those who aspire to leadership embrace our power to use what is - to create what can be...with excellence."[15] *[sic]*

4. Presence rocks!

"That's right, Dad [Mum]. If you're not around, your wife [husband] and children will learn to live life without you."
—*Greg Johnson & Mike Yorkey*[16]

Front line | noun | (usu. the front line) • the military line or part of an army that is closest to the enemy

A Leader Must Be in the Front Line

As a leader at home, presence is the key element that will determine relations at home. It drives the identity of your family, the character of your children, and their eventual impact on society. Presence of a leader is at the core of the ethos of community. It provides security to followers and gives them a better sense of belonging. With this brand of active leadership, people begin to understand and answer to the question "Who am I?"

Ideally, the response to this question should default to a very specific point of reference such as a person who is steadfast and reliable. It is like having a GPS with homing coordinates already pre-programmed into it. We should not have to worry whether we will get home. However, I suppose there are many like myself who struggled to find similar conditions growing up. Instead, we may encounter people waiting to invade, take advantage of, or cause destruction of our family members. It is therefore important for the leader to be out in the front to protect the integrity of his family.

Naturally, followers will not do what the leader is not practicing. In fact, human beings, like water, tend to follow the path of least resistance. If they do follow, most probably it is out of fear, not choice. For discipline to work practical examples will have a major influence on your followers. If young children must eat their vegetables, it should be obvious what you need to do: you cannot be chewing on a steak and expect them to plough through a pile of green stuff! It cannot be expected that followers will take the desired action unless the leader walks the plank first, and shows there is nothing to fear at the bottom of the fall.

Steve Jobs is arguably one of the select few people that epitomized presence. He had a unique leadership style, one that helped Apple Inc. transform the way we interact with technology. It was his presence, both in body and spirit. Jay Elliot[17] says the following of the man:

"Who would say which of the following is more remarkable: That Steve Jobs would not set foot on the Apple campus for another ten years? Or that NeXT computer platform would lay the foundation for the new-generation operating system of the Macintosh? Or that the workstation was designed to sell at a six-figure price point well above the reach of most individuals, it would ultimately redirect Steve toward what would become his ultimate calling – designing for the consumer?

Yet even more important than any of these advances was the corporate culture that he nurtured at NeXT. In what would become the blueprint for Apple, Steve flattened hierarchies, provided generous benefits, reframed staffers as 'members' rather than 'employees', and oversaw an open-plan facility that physically embodied what for him was a new way of working...

Meanwhile, at Apple, Steve was like an invisible presence. Even employees who arrived after he left could not help but feel his imprint. One employee, though she had not met Steve, put it this way: 'I had a sense that it was still his company. There was the same pervasive feeling of pride, energy and passion, and the Steve Jobs story was kept live by the many people who had been under his leadership'." *[sic]*

So what can families borrow from Steve Jobs's leadership style at Apple? Even though he had not set foot on the Apple Inc. Campus for ten years, Steve had been a very present leader years before. He had led from the front, helping product teams mull through challenges and marketing teams with brilliant presentations. He was an all-around manager with a firm grasp of the financial aspects of the company as with the final product his company was producing. Without presence at home, we can't be the leaders our families are entitled to. It becomes paramount that we have a very practical understanding of all facets of our families.

Says James Baldwin, "Children have never been very good

at listening to their elders, but they've never failed to imitate them."[18] When your child is young, most of the leadership you will provide for him or her is by instruction. However, the ballgame dramatically changes when they grow older. Leadership in this phase is by influence only. What do I mean? If you did not have a solid relationship with your child when they were younger, you cannot expect any meaningful connection at this stage. What we sow is what we reap. And you cannot sow from a distance, you must be in the field to plant those seeds; likewise, if you are absent from your child's life, your relationship will never solidify.

Espousing 'I am'

I have had the privilege of watching mountain gorillas in the wild. The first time was in eastern part of the Democratic Republic of Congo and in Rwanda the second time round. These beasts are a wonder to behold in real life. Mountain gorilla families can only have one leader at any one time. The silverback, the alpha male, can be easily identified by silver fur on his back. He is majestic and his dominance is unmistakable. All other males are completely black and pay allegiance to the silverback, as do the females and children. If an external attack visits a gorilla family, the silverback would lead in fighting off the enemies. His family members take comfort in the fact that they belong to his family, and that he will take care of them.

"The silverback is the center of the troop's attention, making all the decisions, mediating conflicts, determining the movements of the group, leading the others to feeding sites and taking responsibility for the safety and well-being of the troop. Younger males subordinate to the silverback, known as blackbacks, may serve as backup protection."[19]

Something different happens when parents take up intentional leadership at home. They set aside time for play, talk, and reading.

The family cooks, shops, and dreams as a team. They laugh, cry, and reminisce together. They become one, a family with a common identity, though the characteristics of individual family members will vary. Due to this tight bond, the family becomes the true north for members, the one constant they can rely on in a chaotic world, especially during times of conflict or pain, as well as joy and celebration.

As the individuals have developed a sense of identity, how they react can be clearly referenced to a particular brand. That family brand is a culmination of an identity development process, a common set of values, practices, behavior and beliefs that the family subscribes to. This brand differentiates one family from another and positions a family within the broader community. As children grow in the cusp of the family brand, it is has a significant influence on them. It guides them as they grow up and develop their own personalities. The children's personal brands evolve over time and are heavily influenced by the family brand that surrounded them.

My wife and I have a mentor couple—Anzaya and Mbithe—that helped influence the parenting of our wonderful children. They facilitated a a parenting course we attended when we were five months into our first pregnancy. One foundational piece of advice they gave us, just before our first child was born was this: "Bring up your child in such a way that when they are old enough, it is the value of hurting your relationship with them that will keep them on the right path." The urgency of making sure that our family was the core of our children's identities came into sharp focus. We mapped out ways to cement our relationship with our child (my wife was 5-months pregnant with our first-born), a practice that we do not intend to deviate from anytime soon.

When our oldest children were five and two years old, respectively, my wife came up with an ingenious way to cement our identity. On some poster paper, she wrote the following creed, which was then hung on the first-floor landing of our home:

The Kimunya Creed

We are one [unity].
We defend each other [when others gang up against us].
We support each other [teach, learn, make time].
We cheer each other [celebrate each other, together].
We lift each other up [during difficult times].
We finish a job we have started [resilience, perseverance].
We do not follow the crowd [peer pressure].
We obey our parents [follow wholesome instructions].

Even now, when one of our children goes off the rail, all we have to ask them is, "Are you a Kimunya?" Their response is instinctive, as they know who they are and what that brand stands for. They have an identity not only in name, but in the behaviors and beliefs they should espouse..

For my leadership to be effective, my team, i.e. my family, must have one mind, one heart, and one voice. This alignment reminds me of when one wheel on my car became out of balance. Everything was honky-dory until I hit a certain speed. Then the whole car began to rattle. The ride became very uncomfortable and it was difficult to concentrate on driving. The vibrations were transmitted from the front wheels to the steering wheel. Instinctively, I gripped hard on the wheel and this only made the already bad situation worse! My hands screamed for relief. I wanted out!

If I am not in tune with my family, my engagement with them ends up like the car described above. When there are no problems among us, we cruise along easily. We may not take enough time to assess if everything is okay before the ride becomes uncomfortable. However, let conflict, tension or difficulties arise. Then, our relationships unravel and our existence becomes strained. Like the car out of alignment, we soon realize that mending fences is far more challenging

Unfortunately, many families do not take time to invest in their brand. It's therefore not surprising to see families breaking up, children are abandoned, and social anarchy is prevalent. Families are desperate because they have no sense of identity, no ideals. I have had one parent too many declare that they will cross the bridge when they come to it. Do not wait to cross the bridge! Why not build it instead? That way you will determine your own destiny and chart out your family's path to the future.

Create Your Family Identity

When they are still young, your children will derive their identity from you. You are their superhero. It is not a surprise, then, that all they want to be when they grow up is "Like Daddy!" or "Like Mummy!" You are their universe. They have leaned to trust you for their nourishment, care, love and protection. As you interact with them, they begin to identify with you and align themselves to your actions and behavior.

Before you start creating an identity in your children, it is very important that you fully appreciate the context you yourself grew up in. Your past will have a significant impact on how you develop the culture that fuels the engine that drives your own family. I struggled to create a culture for my own family. Although my intention was noble, the harder I tried, the more frustrating the whole process became. At one point, I was ready to throw in the towel until I came to a realization that blew my mind away. All along, I was using my head-knowledge and not digging deep into my soul to understand the skeletons in my closet.

My leadership was already compromised even before I got to the starting blocks. The track was littered with obstacles; I only had the luxury of making one qualifying run. And it had to be straight to the tape.

Now, let me illustrate how significant the stakes against me were by going down memory lane. Becoming a teenager was a very significant milestone for my mates and I. When boys turned this age, it was a time to proudly (and publicly) demonstrate one's transition from childhood to manhood. It was also a watershed period just before we headed out to high school. It was boy's season; my neighborhood was abuzz with poignant talk of boys-to-men, of the initiation.

It was glorious December, school was out and the crops had been harvested and the produce in storage. Christmas was around the corner. And above all, before Christmas Day rolled into town, I was about to become a man. Joy, oh what joy… I eagerly waited for my father to come home from his 'busy' workplace in some far-flung town. And I waited and waited.

Finally the wait was over. My mother woke me up very early in the morning to get ready for the great day that lay ahead of me. At 5 A.M., it was chilly and still dark outside. My mother and I headed off to the surgery clinic some twenty-odd minutes away from home. By 6 A.M., the initiation procedure complete, I headed back home a man. However, I trudged home with my head hung low in shame, glad that none of my mates was out of bed at this early morning hour. In my community, it is the role of the boy's father—uncle or grandfather if the father was deceased—to take the son through this amazing transition from childhood to manhood. Yet my father, who was supposed to usher me into his world, was nowhere to be found. What type of father would abandon his son at that pivotal period in his life, leaving him alone as he graduated into manhood? As much as I did not want to accept it, I had only been transformed into a bruised man. The physical pain of the circumcision procedure paled in comparison to the incessant bleeding in depths of my soul.

As always, my ever-present mother was all I had going for me. As much as I loved her dearly, what sane boy was going to share tales of his *mother* taking him through his initiation? Who in their right mind would dare welcome the inevitable ridicule from his peers? I had to bottle up the pain in my heart and present a cover story to my mates as we narrated our different experiences. Branded with this fractured self-identity, I went through my teenage years bruised, broken, and feeling like an outright reject.

But deep inside the very core of my being something still stirred. I vowed this would not happen again on my watch. The family tree was just about to receive some serious pruning. This led me to make some radical decisions down the road. When my wife and I were seven months into our first pregnancy, I was offered a new job. Now, that was great news; with a new mouth to feed, a better paycheck was most welcome. At the end of the job interview, they asked if I had any questions or comments. My response was thus: "I have a young family, and our baby is due any time. I just wanted you to know that when my family squeaks, I will jump. They are my first priority." You should have seen the baffled looks on their faces! It was like I had just walked into the dentist's with a major cavity in my tooth while chewing on candy. Although I thought I had blown my chances with my comment, I got the job offer within a week! I signed the contract with pride.

I would provide an identity for my family. My job would not keep me away from my loved ones. Precious time was going to be invested in them. We would grow together; my children would have the presence of their father, and my wife of her husband.

If you want to see your personal brand grow, and to help others develop their own brands, make this same commitment, and follow through. "Be the change you want to see in the world," Mahatma Gandhi challenges us.

To create my family's identity, I have had to make radical

choices, as well as adjustments as the world has thrown ever-changing situations our way. It was challenging to begin with, but like a baker making a unique and wonderful dessert, I started by recognizing that I needed crucial ingredients for my family's *cake*.

Let us explore this in more detail.

Ingredient #1–Dare to Discipline

For one thing, I had to set up clearly understood discipline standards that were shared and embraced by the whole family. These standards were clear on what the consequences were of contravening the code of discipline in our home. My wife and I also had to be diligent enough to follow through with the necessary pre-defined corrective measures. However, I also have to invest in quality time with my family if these standards are to last. I have to love enough to provide my family with discipline, and to clamp down on indiscipline when it rears its ugly head. *Good* fathers only step in when their children go astray. *Great* fathers set the standard (the rules), enlighten their children on the consequences of breaking those standards, and enforce disciplinary measures when the standards are breached. This tough love cares not only for the present situation, but also for the child's very soul to eternity.

Why is discipline important? Why should you stress yourself with this bothersome, time-consuming, insanity-inducing process? Think with me through the following scenario.

A chubby, cute and gummy grin greets me as I walk into our family living room. In a fuzzy blur, a bundle of bright clothing comes hurtling toward me. Before my tired mind can instruct my fatigue-plagued muscles to get out of the way, my lovely child is upon me. "Daddy!" the joy-filled squeal erupts. After some cuddles, play, and fun, it is time to eat, bathe, and then go to sleep. (You could substitute these tasks for anything else that the child needed to do [for their own good, of course] according to my specific instructions). Then a transformation suddenly descends on the child: their face contorts and the mouth morphs into a blood-curdling scream that emanates from the depths of their lungs. It is hard to fathom how such tiny lungs could possibly generate that many decibels! Now the whole neighborhood must know that all is not well in my home!

Boy did I dread those moments of madness. How I reacted, or did not, determined how my child would turn out in the future. I could choose to respond in one of two ways: ignore the tantrum or discipline the child.

The first, and easier, option was to ignore the tantrum. This was easy to justify: he would yell himself to sleep anyway. Other times, I gave in to the demands, just to get the child to shut up. "He is just a child," I would convince myself, "He will get over this behavior when he gets older."

As I contemplated my next move, I projected this behavior into the future. I remembered a thought shared with my wife and I by our mentors, whose three children were teenagers at the time. "Fast track your lovely child to their teenage years. The tantrums you see now in your toddler will become more amplified, and transform into truancy," they informed us before they quickly threw a spanner into the works: "As an adult, how would these cute tantrums pan out?" Will your child quit their job just because they don't like their boss or a colleague? Or if they break the law, will they bribe and talk their way out of the fix?

By not dealing with a disciplinary issue in any of my children, I could be setting the stage for failure in the future. Am I creating the perfect storm? My children may turn out to be brilliant in their academics, but mediocre in self-control and morals, or devoid of any spiritual life.

In essence, without discipline, children will be totally lost and incompetent to engage in a positive manner with their external environment. They will be perfect candidates for adverse peer pressure. The world could be theirs to conquer, but who could do so in a rudderless, leaky, sail-less dinghy. They will not be in control of their being, but governed by their immature desires, or, worse, by the priorities of other people.

Love enough to discipline and follow through is what I keep reminding myself. I can be a good father who only steps in when my children go astray. However, I strive to be a *great* father. This relationship can only be built on basic critical essentials that include unreserved love for my spouse, quality time spent together, and being a good role model.

Ingredient #2–Tackle Indiscipline Head-on

It is all in the mind. When it comes to indiscipline, many parents are surprised to realize that a major proportion of blame lies with them and not the child. To the child, everything they encounter is new. Children must be taught the correct way to react to every new experience and situation. The child needs to be immersed into a culture of discipline for them to know what indiscipline is and its consequences.

For my child to be disciplined, I have to lead by example. I can't expect my son or daughter to clean up after whatever odyssey they have just been engaged in when I continuously leave a trail of destruction everywhere I go. Fortunately, I choose to correct and train the errant child. I have to take leadership over the development of my child. They need a father who is firm enough to direct them towards the right path, the path of discipline. This is a challenging choice to make. To correct and train our children, some critical factors have to come into play: time, love, and carefully crafted ground rules.

A few months before the birth of our first child, my wife and

I were blessed to sit at the feet of Anzaya and Mbithe (a wonderful couple mentioned in the previous chapter). They taught us the ropes of parenting. We engaged with them through this instruction and observed how they brought up their own children. Their children were well behaved, socially adjusted, and seemed to be having a lot of fun in the process. What seemed improbable became a possibility when our own children were of age.

We chose to do our best to work on our children's consciences. This conscience would guide them to have self-control, respect for authority, obedience, and to adhere to rules, as well as help them accede to receiving correction when they have stepped out of line.

In *Growing Kids God's Way*, Gary and Anne Marie Ezzo provide a great insight into your child's conscience:

"Indeed, from the age of three years and up begin to acquire a functioning conscience, controlled by a developing system of beliefs, ideas, values and virtues that internally decree what is right, wrong, good, or evil. This is what determines how one should respond to situations…

This special something acts as the silent voice stirring within the heart; monitoring conduct for moral accountability… The destiny of a child's life is shaped by his conscience. The human conscience actually functions at two levels of existence–a lower and higher conscience. The lower conscience contains the innate sense of right and wrong, which all humanity shares. The higher conscience is subject to training and receives the specific standards or right and wrong formed by beliefs and values.

All parents have a social obligation to train their children in community values. With their moral pen, they write a prescription of right and wrong, what to do and what not to do, and all the moral reasons why and why not. Since parents offer instruction both by precept and example, attention must be paid not only to what moral truth is imparted to a child, but how it is imparted".[20] *[sic]*

It is this higher level of conscience that discipline endeavors to address. Several steps must be in place if discipline and conscience are to develop in a child.

First, I needed to teach my children self-control, an art where they master their body and bring it under control. Essentially, self-control prevents "a deception develops which appeals to the appetites and pride that leaves us vulnerable to destructive habits. Eventually it limits your potential and leads to misery,"[21] advise Anzaya & Mbithe. I am therefore called to train my child to have both emotional and physical self-control. The child should be able to do *what* I instruct them to do, *when* they are required, *where* the instruction is given, and *how* I prefer. Examples of physical self-control are eating, bathing, sleeping, playing, etc. Emotional self-control is the balance between impulse and restraint, desire and willpower, gratification and delay.

Secondly, my children needed to understand and appreciate the value of being under an authority. My wife and I are the first authority for our children. However, we represent other external authorities that our children will be subject to: God, government, school, and others. If my children cannot submit to my authority in a healthy way, will they respect any other authority? I believe the possibility is very slim! They will be at the forefront of breaking common law, and any decent engagement with society is unlikely. They will not only be a pain to me, no one else will want them around.

Let me illustrate this with an event that will forever be embedded in my mind. One Saturday afternoon, my family and I were lounging, catching up on reading and sports. At about three o'clock, we received a call from some friends who wanted to come and visit. Suddenly, with military precision, we all piled into the car and went for a long drive. You see, some few weeks before, the same family had visited us with some cataclysmic results. By the time they left, one door was hanging off its hinges and our son's tricycle had been broken up into six pieces. We did not want to hang out with such people. In our thoughts, we associated with them with the hurt they had left behind. Not to mention that we had to buy our son another bike!

Despite being warned of dire consequences if they did not follow instructions, those other kids still left a trail of destruction in their wake. They just would not submit to authority! Although this was a somewhat traumatizing experience, there was a good lesson for our children in the matter. They now began to respond better to our authority as well as appreciate the need for the same. They realized that not following our instruction and guidance brings destruction and pain to everyone, not just to the perpetrator.

Third, we make rules that govern the way our children practice self-control and respond to authority. Order, harmony, and peace need to be found in our home, it is our refuge, where we retreat to recharge our batteries and lick our wounds after engaging with a harsh world. Rules help our children to understand what is expected of them and the consequences that will fall upon them when they choose to disregard those rules. These rules provide a structure and boundaries, inside which they can thrive. This structure now has been extended to anyone who visits our peace-loving home. All are subject to these boundaries, from my children's grandparents to their friends.

For discipline to work, there must be well-delineated consequences for disregard of the rules of engagement. Now before you go off the handle, please note this is not your license to beat up your child. Discipline has to be administered with love. Only then can it have meaning and the intended effect. If carried out otherwise, it only yields resentment and the deep urge to escape.

Ingredient #3—Invest in Precious Memories

If my life were an investment account, there would be more withdrawals than deposits. Looking back, I can count the number of great memories together with my parents and siblings on my fingers We hardly had anything of note in terms of great memories. I can't remember any special birthday meals or cards. There was hardly anything deposited in my memory bank. It is during close family activities that satisfying and affirming relationships are built. Memorable moments

Why is developing precious memories with our children important? They help to lay the emotional and relational foundations crucial to building self-esteem. As I grew older, I faced periods of low-self esteem.

At the end of the day, I realize that it does not matter how much money I bring home. Will a big paycheck keep my family together? Well, a well-padded pocket would not hurt anyone... or could it? My family would live a happy life, one devoid of the want that I had to contend with when I was growing up. Exotic destinations would become our backyards; wafting barbeques of delicious, choice cuts our everyday meal. But whenever I am tempted to dwell on this fantasy, reality swiftly jolts me back to my senses. It is true, I have to make deposits into those around me, but the paychecks I have to draw will not carry any monetary value. Rather, they are written in terms such as 'love,' 'care,' 'time,' 'sacrifice,' and all such values that bring people closer together, and whose worth never diminish over time.

In a *Reader's Digest* article titled "Hard Truths About Day Care," the dangers of withdrawing your presence from your child is brought into sharp focus. "What the very young want, and urgently need, child-development experts agree, is not education or socialization, but the affection and unhurried attention of their parents. The deepest problem with paid child-rearing is that someone is being asked to do for money what very few of us are able to do for any other than love."

Small sacrifices have to be made along the way as you build memories with those you love. Michael Henry Sr. sums it up so well when he says that as we invest in the future together we're part of something worthwhile that's uniquely valuable.

My positive memories of growing up are as rare as the displaying of a diamond in a rough neighborhood. The most consistent memories that help cement me with my family stop before I turned ten. After that, life was just about existence. My poor mum tried hard to create some good times for us, but with hardly any support from my father and four kids to care for, I guess she was in survival mode too.

I know some of you may take it for granted that you have great memories of your childhood. I am still floored when I hear people reminiscing about their childhood with laughter and joy. If you had the opportunity to do amazing things with your family, you were blessed! Now make a commitment to pass those same types of blessings along to the next generation, so they may in turn have precious memories of childhood when they are grown. We should all strive to build legacies of love, joy, and commitment.

Leadership calls me to become more deliberate in the stories and experiences I deposit into my children's memory bank. Every night, I have to trudge up the stairs three times. Not that I am working out – although this is a side benefit! No, I am giving my three kids piggyback rides to bed. You should see the twinkle in their eyes and smiles on their faces! They will hop up and down in anticipation. I cannot wait to hear their stories about this when they are all grown up.

One Saturday morning, I woke up early with my then four-year-old son. The girls—my wife and two daughters—slept on. We quietly showered and dressed, then snuck out of the house. The boys were out on a secret mission: head to the local store for some bread, milk, and eggs. The thirty minutes we spent together that morning filled his tank to overflowing. By sunset, he had narrated the escapade to my wife and his twenty-year-old cousin repeatedly! We connected, and in his mind, we were heroes, fulfilling a quest as epic as any bedtime story.

I had provided him with a memorable moment. His reserve tank of positivity had just received a top up from which he could hopefully draw when he would encounter a rough patch in future. This extremely positive experience didn't even require any real sacrifice or effort on my part (someone was going to have to go to the store, regardless). But by making the small choice to take him along, I did not only complete this errand, but I gave my son an amazing adventure along the way.

Looking back to the *Reader's Digest* article mentioned before, all it took to make my son's day was my presence, and the inclusion of him in my task.

Eating healthy is another way to create memorable moments. "Eating?" you ask! Growing up with so little, I learned what it is to have very limited choice over the food in the pantry. Mum tried to spruce our meals up as much as she could with what she had, but to be honest, there was very little, in both quantity and variety. I craved for nice juicy steaks, eggs, pasta, and many more goodies, but meat was a luxury, and even though we had a few chickens, those were currency to be sold off during lean times. I vividly remember eating pumpkins until we were nearly orange in the face! Boy did I hate pumpkins! They were simple to grow and they store easily for long periods. At one point, I discovered how to hasten the rotting process. All that was needed was to break off the small stalk that remained after they were harvested. A few days later, rot would set in from the inside! Mum could not comprehend why her precious cargo rotted so fast, until my disclosure years later when I was in college.

When I got my first well-paying job, the temptation was to make up for lost opportunities. I would eat out on a regular basis. One day, I sat down to evaluate my lifestyle. In the process, I realized that the money I was spending on unnecessary and unhealthy eat-outs consumed about a tenth of my salary. Needless to say, I stopped! Slowly, I started eating fresh, homemade food. When the children came along, I took the time to introduce them to cooking. We would, and still do, don our aprons and spin a wicked meal.

From birth, all our three of our children help with shopping for groceries, fruits, and vegetables. When they were younger all they did was tag along. The eldest is now seven years, and we are slowly bringing her up to speed with making shopping lists. Besides creating memorable moments together, shopping has helped them take leadership of what they eat. We were amazed when one day our girl and boy attended a birthday party. They went along with our friend. When they came back, our friend was gob smacked. Apparently, our kids – then four and two – had refused to take any soda and demanded for "live" juice as they call freshly squeezed juice. As none was available, they chose to take water. That was inspirational!

"Your child will face countless disappointments in future. Friendships, work relationships, and romantic entanglements all provide opportunities for doubt. Your child's life will be filled with uncertainties, but you don't have to be one of them [uncertainties]. Make sure your child has no reason to doubt you. Are you worthy of your child's trust? Does he or she know that no matter how fearful life becomes, Dad [and Mum] will be there to love, accept, help, and guide?"[22] note Gary & Anne Marie Ezzo in *Growing Kid's God Way.*

Remember, to bake your *family cake* and cement its identity, you will require to balance creating precious memories, laying the ground for proper discipline and finally, having the courage to tackle indiscipline that may crop up.

Fathers Needed

My very good friend, confidant, and advisor Peter Mutua put this very well in an article he wrote in Kenya's *Business Daily.*[23] He was exploring how the lack of role models harms business and society. This is what the article expounded...

In the year 2000, the warden in charge of Hluluwe-Umfolozi Game Reserve in South Africa had a problem. In fact, he had thirty-six big problems. That was the number of rhinoceroses killed in Umfolozi over the previous two years, with thirteen of those deaths coming in the last five months of 1999. This was a serious setback to the park's efforts to restore the decimated population of rhinos. What alarmed the warden was not so much the rhinos' deaths as the manner in which they had been killed. Some had broken backs while others had been gored to death. None had their horns hacked off, a typical sign of poaching. Given that rhinos weigh about two tons, what or who was responsible for these bizarre deaths?

The warden was at pains to explain this and in a state of near panic. It did not make any sense at all. Just as they were about to engage the services of a *sangoma* (a traditional witchdoctor) to divine the cause of the misfortune, a game warden in a helicopter was treated to a very disturbing scene: a young elephant bull was in hot pursuit of a male rhinoceros. The elephant was repeatedly trying to mount the smaller creature! The distraught rhino tried to flee from the overtures, to no avail. The young bull finally caught up with the rhino and forcibly mounted it, breaking the rhino's back in the process. For good measure, the elephant gored the fallen rhino with its tusks, as if to punctuate its conquest. Shocking as this scene was, it explained the strange happenings in the game reserve.

But what had precipitated this unusual behavior? It started in the 1990s with the culling of elephants in Kruger National Park. Orphaned elephants from Kruger were moved to Hluluwe-Umfolozi and Pilanesburg game reserves. Nothing had been heard of them until these unusual incidents in Umfolozi.

Now that the park managers knew what was causing the deaths, they devised a plan: they introduced big mature bulls into the reserve. As soon as the young bull elephants saw the gigantic mature bulls, they calmed down immediately. They gravitated around the big, majestic bulls, imitating their every move. The rhino massacre came to an abrupt end and peace has reigned over the whole expanse of Umfolozi since.

What lessons can family leaders learn from this story? Without the appropriate role models or examples, young males—whether human or animal—will often run amok, with disastrous outcomes to their community. The young bulls manifested their strength by killing rhinos. Young men react by embracing such vices as burning schools, shooting their peers, abusing alcohol and other prohibited substances, and forming criminal gangs, to name a few examples. While this miscreant behavior should be condemned, official statements, government-sanctioned crackdown, or prohibitive legislation can rarely contain it.

So what should the leader in the family do to address upheaval in the community? Most importantly, we need to recognize that young men in our communities yearn for responsible male role models that they can look up to and emulate. They are crying for attention, desperate to be shepherded. To become a role model to the young men around me, I need to become more secure in both my inherent position in society and myself. It is only then that I can provide leadership to my community.

As parents, we have been very deliberate and actively present in our children's lives. We have been able to practice what Lyn Boyer refers to as 'Affective Leadership': the ability to connect with and influence other people to achieve common goals through strong and genuine relationships and emotional attachments.

For my wife and I, a primary function of intentional leadership at home is to develop culture. For the right culture to emerge, deliberate and careful nurturing is required. In *Outliers: The Story of Success*, Malcolm Gladwell notes that people do not rise from nothing. "[People] are invariably the beneficiaries of hidden advantages and extraordinary opportunities and cultural legacies that allow them to learn and work hard and make sense of the world in ways others cannot."[24]

As a leader, I heed the lessons all around me that teach me how to develop and improve the culture that I am responsible for. Culture that, when brought together, provides direction and hope for my family and the human race in general.

5. Evaluate

"At some point in your life, you will face a situation where you are in a leadership position and dozens – maybe thousands or millions – look to you to lead. When that occurs, you won't feel ready. But you have to lead anyway."
—*Oliver Van DeMille*

Take stock | noun | make an overall assessment of a particular situation

Take Stock

Leading at home can often be frustrating, and may leave you feeling incapacitated. You end up like a deer caught in headlights, without any idea where to run or hide. You feel weak, scared, and lost. This dilemma becomes especially complicated when no solution or fix is at hand. You are coasting along the highway, bopping your head to some cool vibes and thinking all is well, then… Wham! Without warning, you are sailing through the air, flying in a car designed to be on terra firma, full of dread of the moment you crash back down to earth.

It, therefore, becomes paramount that every leader takes some time out to evaluate their current state of affairs. Leadership is all about your understanding of the present situation in relation to your history and future (vision). This does not come easily and you have to constantly adjust your sails to capitalize the most out of the wind powering your boat. You will have to learn new skills that will enable you to relate appropriately with your growing family. For example, what worked for your two-year old toddler will not resonate with them when they become teenagers.

Like a rally car, you cannot expect the tires used on tarmac road to be effective on muddy, off-road tracks. The vehicle and engine may remain the same one on both terrains, but you need off-road tires to get the best out of your driving experience when out in the bush.

Leadership and parenting have one common feature: quality time is needed if anything is to be passed on to the next generation. The educator may use this time to demonstrate how a tool works, guide on practical life skills, cultivate positive ethics and a willingness to work hard, as well as nurture the young mind and establish how social interaction works. Masterpieces inspire the apprentice towards refined skill. A leader will not have any impact unless they establish—for both themselves and their followers—that values can only be imparted over time.

I have had to value myself to be able to gauge my leadership level, without which I cannot evaluate my leadership potential. Without knowing my potential, I was not able to become the leader I was meant to be. Taking heed of the lessons all around me, including in my family, guide me on how to develop and improve my value. These are the values guide my principles or standards of behavior as well as my judgment of what is important in life. I then can confidently take up my role as a father, husband and member of my community.

If your leadership style is hands-off, you guide your family on what is required of them. The focus is on the "bare minimum" expectation you have of them. Your interaction with them is reactive, which makes it incumbent on *them* to drive their relationships with you. You only become available when they encounter any challenges that require 'informed' guidance from you, the team captain.

The flipside is the hands-on style, the micro-manager. You constantly look over your family members' shoulders, fearing they might deviate from your perfect way. In this case, your family reacts *to* you rather than engaging *with* you.

I chose to adopt a hybrid of these two leadership styles. It is what I refer to as a responsible leadership. This leadership style is more oriented towards specific outcomes while having a focus on confronting and overcoming the obstacles. In between the outcomes and the obstacles is teamwork and building relationships with my family. It is where precious memories are developed.

Build a Healthy Culture

It is time to shift gears, time to jettison the past. A change is required of your leadership. You need to constantly re-calibrate your style to accommodate the prevailing environment. You are a team, and to win, all members have to be on the same page.

A crisis can cause a whole lot of self-doubt in a leader. You may feel lonely, and even have no one to turn to for help or advice. You will need to find a few people who can become your bouncing wall. These are your accountability partners that help you check on your progress, or lack thereof. They provide solid advice and, when needed, loving rebuke. If you are to succeed as a leader, you need to establish your personal *Board of Directors*. Remember, it can be very lonely as a leader, and you need all the credible support you can find.

Remember that leadership mostly operates like our daily nutrition. For our bodies to grow and repair themselves from the rigors of life, our meals need to be balanced and carefully planned (proteins, carbohydrates, vitamins, etc.). We can't to eat one huge meal and expect it to take us through a whole week. Likewise, the leadership process is measured, targeted, and carefully thought through. Andrew Carnegie notes this: "And here is the prime condition of success, the great secret. Concentrate your energy, thoughts and capital exclusively upon the business in which you are engaged in. Having begun in one line, resolve to fight it out on that line; to lead in it. Adopt every improvement, have the best machinery and know the most about it,"[25] When hunting, your prey keeps on shifting its position. It is incumbent on you to change your approach to be successful in leading.

Finally, leadership is a journey, not the destination. Invest in knowledge. A true leader maintains a ravenous hunger to learn, as this is the only way to ensure sustainable growth. The moment you stop learning, your hang up your gloves on leadership. A leader is forever thirsty for knowledge, restless with status quo and always challenging himself to become better at what he does. Your followers will notice this dedication to self-improvement and most probably will embrace it in their own lives too.

Unless a person is ready to change himself, no amount of money, concepts, techniques, or gizmos invested in them will work any magic. "People cannot be educated unless they choose to seek education, and they seek it when they are inspired by great teachers, past and present,"[26] writes Olivier Van DeMille. The type of relationship between a teacher [leader] and student [follower] governs any individual's development. This holds true for leadership. It does not matter how great a leader I may be, if my vision does not excite my followers, then my mission is nothing but a lame duck that will never find its wings!

I therefore propose that two key ingredients—to *teach* and to *inspire*—become necessary to take any leadership to the desired levels. And for me to become an effective leader, I have to seriously integrate them as principle building blocks of my approach to leading.

Teach... Don't Only Focus on Educating

In *Stop Stealing Dreams*, Seth Godin says, "Leadership is the most important trait for players in the connected revolution. Leadership involves initiative, and in the connected world, nothing happens until you step up and begin... And as the world changes even faster, we don't reward people who can slavishly follow yesterday's instructions. All of the value to the individual (and to the society she belongs to) goes to the individual who can draw a new map, who can solve a problem that didn't even exist yesterday."[27]

If people are not aware of how to think, then they will never learn. This is the main distinguishing feature between teaching and educating. To teach is all about causing someone to learn or understand something by example or experience. It is relational Educating on the other hand is the process of giving intellectual, moral, and social instruction to someone typically at a school or university.

To become a great leader, my leadership has to adopt two

principles that foster a teaching environment: being a mentor, and learning from the classics.

As a *mentor*, I constantly have to interface directly with my followers. They have to see and feel me. However, I also need to remain extremely focused, so that the small details do not derail me from the goal. I also have to learn to step back when my follower begins to make connections on his or her own. The idea is to consistently encourage a process of self-discovery. According to Mortimer J. Alder, "...learning which results in expanded knowledge and improved understanding (rather than memorized facts) is essentially a process of discovery, the teacher's art consists largely in devices whereby one individual can help another to lift himself up from a state of knowing and understanding less to knowing and understanding more."[28]

An effective leader will always turn to principles, methods, and practices developed by legendary teachers past and present. Thus, my leadership has to be fed by the second principle, *classics*. "It is chiefly through books that we enjoy intercourse with superior minds... In the best books, great men talk to us, give us their most precious thoughts, and pour their souls into ours,"[29] notes William Ellery Channing. I can then adopt the wisdom I obtain from these studies to refine and propel my ability to lead. Only by immersing myself into the greatness of the classics can I then become successful in leading others.

Inspire

To inspire, I need to spend the time to help my followers understand how to think. If they know how to think, then it sets them on the journey to become effective leaders themselves.

My greatest challenge, therefore, is to understand my followers. Once I understand them, I can then customize my engagement with each individual member of my family in order to creatively encourage him or her to personally pursue leadership. They then will begin to understand that hard work becomes necessary to transform their thoughts into reality. Innovation becomes their driving force and this helps derive the change desperately needed to improve them, to engage humanity towards greatness. "We need inspiration…to build our nation we must exceed all our expectations."[30] Great leaders inspire people to heights they thought never existed, to realms reserved for legends.

I therefore, have to constantly be on the lookout for the great potential in others. Not only should I readily point this potential out to them, but I should also be willing to pay the cost of helping them to apply that potential toward noble service to humanity. William Arthur Ward said, "The mediocre teacher tells; the good teacher explains; the superior teacher demonstrates; the great teacher inspires."[31]

Motivational expert Zig Ziglar describes some of the teachers he had in his life: "My first-grade teacher, Mrs. Dement Warren, taught me to read. My sixth-grade teacher, Mr. J.K. Worley, taught me to love to read. I'm convinced parents should let their children see them reading good books, magazines, and articles. Children are great imitators. If they see their parents wrapped up in a good book instead of glued on the television set, they are likely to follow suit. In addition, read good books to your kids. Please consider it, parents. Show your love for reading and your kids will do the same."[32] What a wonderful call to action!

Our three children bear very different personalities. Our first girl is ambitious, spontaneously happy-go-lucky and unfazed; our boy is a kind-hearted perfectionist who will not flow with the gang; and the youngest girl is our family organizer, meticulous to crossing the T's and dotting the I's. Yet, one characteristic that is undeniable in all of them is a genuine love for reading. The moment they learned how to read their first word is one the greatest skills they have received so far. They are all performing at a reading level of children up to three years older than themselves. The youngest – just turned three years – brandished her favorite book and confidently declared to her mother, "I want to read for myself now. Mama, please teach me how to read!" Was this peculiar? No it was not. Her siblings, now seven and five, had made similar demands at around the same age. They are now proficient in reading and comprehension. Greek mythology, *The Chronicles of Narnia, Around the World in Eighty Days, Gifted Hands* (by Dr. Ben Carson)—these are just a few of the works of literature my children have engaged with so far.

This love for reading that my children have did not come about by chance. The adventure with books began well before they breathed their first breaths. When my wife was about five-to-six months into each of the three pregnancies, we started reading to them. This provided for a very interesting scene: reading a kiddy story to a bump! Reading became a ritual, a privilege extended to them to this day. Not only do my wife and I read to our children, we also read great books ourselves. Thus, we have set an example by showing them how we spend our valuable time. It is therefore not surprising that when they take some rest, they will seek out a book to keep them company.

Reading not only helps our children seek out knowledge, it also provides them with the confidence to engage with their external environment. When our first daughter was five, she visited the Kenya National Library Service's main facility to attend a children's club. This was her first time ever to the library. The first activity of the day was poetry, and the club's coordinator asked for a child volunteer to teach the others a poem. There was a poignant unease as none of the children wanted to go up on stage. Suddenly, a hand shot up. It was our precious six-year-old daughter. My poor wife nearly fell off her seat in fright! She wondered what our daughter could possibly teach her peers. Before my wife could react, our daughter bounced onto the stage. In a clear, confident voice, and without skipping a beat, she recited the following:

"Peter Piper picked a peck of pickled peppers, a peck of pickled peppers Peter Piper picked. If Peter Piper picked a peck of pickled peppers, where is the peck of pickled peppers Peter Piper picked?"

Immediately, all the children chimed in together and asked to learn the piece. At the end of it, there were many smiling, albeit tongue-tied, children. Curious to know what drove her to volunteer, I asked her and she responded, "It was the right thing to do!" She had this funny look on her that seemed to suggest that I might be growing a little soft in the head. Then it struck me: unbeknownst to her, she was already honing her leadership skills. Without fear of failure, she took the initiative, and taught her peers. Immediately, it took me back to a poem I had seen on Todd Nielsen's blog, *A Slice of Leadership*. In a blog titled 'The Leadership/Parenting Analogy,' Nielsen shared 'Children Learn What They Live' by Dorothy Law Nolte, PhD. Four lines stood out…

"If children live with encouragement, they learn confidence/ If children live with acceptance, they learn to love/ If children live with sharing, they learn generosity/ If children live with security, they learn to have faith in themselves and in those about them."

Remembering these lines helped me to fully appreciate our daughter's response. My wife and I have sung, spoken, and read to our three children even when they were snug in their mother's belly. Through this a culture was incubated, one of care, reading, love, and sharing. No one taught our daughter the tongue twister she recited that morning. Her mother had written it out on a card and posted it on a door at home.

However, my wife and I were still searching on how we can inspire our kids to great achievements without pushing them so hard that they get frustrated and give up, or grow resentful of the pressure. One way we have tried to do this is to accompany their reading with real adventures. For example, after we finished reading Black Beauty, we visited a horse stable. Together with their friends and other parents, we cleaned the stables, and fed, watered and groomed the horses.

Manage Behavior Change

Do you believe that what happens in Vegas truly stays in Vegas? In real life, in parenting, what happens in Vegas is broadcast everywhere else too!

Consistency is critical when it comes to dealing with bad behavior. It is expected of my children to be respectful, kind, compassionate, and well behaved wherever they are. However, I need to be there when a negative influence attacks them. They need to know that I've got their back. Therefore, when in public, if I see another child go off the hook, I will at least go to them and tell them a firm no! I do not discriminate between my children and their friends, or strangers' children. They will all be expected to act and behave with respect, regardless of whether we are at home or in a public area.

The net effect is that my children stop viewing the negative influence around them as a *cool* thing. My hope and prayer is that they get to understand that negative influence is all around them. What matters is how they respond to it, and that greatness lies in rising above mediocrity.

One day, as I was enjoying a cup of coffee before a flight, I had the privilege to watch a group of soldiers at the boarding gate. They must have been on a United Nations peace-building mission. There were over one hundred soldiers, and when they queued up, the queue soon bundled up. Instinctively, starting from the top of the queue, every soldier placed his right hand on his mate's right shoulder and pushed back half an arm's length. Order was restored in the queue.

Soon thereafter, there was a boarding gate change and the same soldiers had to relocate to another gate. Did they all troop helter-skelter to the new gate? Amazingly, they did not! One soft command is all it took for them to about-face and *voila*, the last man on the queue was now at the top. Simply put, it was fun to watch the spectacle.

This coordination did not just happen as if by magic. These soldiers must have undergone a lot of training on how to exhibit disciplined behavior regardless of the external circumstances. What does this teach us about becoming better leaders at home?

First, leadership is all about your understanding of the present situation in relation to not only your history, but also to your Vision for the future. This does not come easily and you have to constantly adjust your sails to capitalize on the wind that is powering your boat. You will have to learn new skills that will enable you to relate appropriately with your growing family. What worked for your two-year-old toddler will not resonate with them when they become teenagers (no matter how much they still behave like two year olds at that point)!

The second lesson I learned that day was about patience. The soldiers were patient with each other as the changes were taking place. They did not squabble, as they knew what was going on was for the good of the team. Remember your family is a team—some members will learn fast or adopt new action readily, others will take some time to appreciate the big picture. It is therefore important that you patiently build their skills, character, and self-esteem.

The third lesson was that their behavior was guided by some common values or standards that were known to all of them. The soldiers were a team, and at that particular moment, they had to work as one to efficiently board onto the aircraft. The same applies to your family. You must provide the leadership that embeds the value-system your family subscribes to. This value system has to be re-visited regularly and fine-tuned to fit the current stage your family is at. Like a rally car, you cannot expect the wheels used on tarmac roads to be effective on muddy, off-road tracks. The vehicle and engine may be the same one on both terrains, but you need off-road tires to get the best out of your driving experience when out in the bush.

Tackles, Cuddles, and Kisses

All human beings crave for affection and touch. I still remember the births of our three children with nostalgia. They were cute and adorable, but above all else, they were vulnerable. The one common thing they had was their desire for touch from my wife and I. When they were sleepy, hungry, in pain, or just happy, all they cared was to be in our hands. We would rock them to sleep, soothe them, and tickle them senseless.

As they grew older, their need for touch changed. Now they wanted to hold our hands as we took walks, or sit on our laps when we read them their storybooks. I remember one time our back yard flooded after a particularly heavy downpour. That evening after work, we all donned our rubber boots and played soccer in the soggy backyard. Water was splashed as we kicked the ball around while squeals of delight bid the setting sun farewell.

Bedtime used to be a delightful affair, as a bedtime story had to be narrated every night. They would wait in anticipation and would not shut their sleepy eyes until a story had been read to them. Now that they read by themselves, I have had to develop a different evening ritual. The girls opt for cuddles and kisses. The boy, on the other hand, wants his goodnight tackle! Goodnight tackle? Yes! He will get into bed and patiently wait for me to come into his room. The excitement on his face is to die for! I will creep up and jump him in a tight tackle. Both of us wrestle briefly and then I bid him goodnight. Ten minutes later, he is out for the count until the following morning.

Why am I sharing this? As a leader, it is critical to constantly evaluate the stage your family is at. This will help you identify any need to re-strategize or develop new activities that will guide your family to the next level.

I was in for a mighty big surprise during the 2012 Christmas season. Every year, our children and their friends stage a Christmas play directed by our wives. This year, it was a little different in that there was a surprise for all the fathers. At the end of the play, a seat was placed on the stage. One by one, each father was called up to the *throne* and *crowned* by his children. They then said something about what they thought of their fathers in front of everyone in the audience. When my turn came along, I was not quite sure what to expect. I knew our three kids had something wonderful for me. The definition of wonderful falls miserably short of what they had in store for me.

At seven years of age, Tinashe *[TEE-nah-shay]*, our eldest, is already amazing us with her level of responsibility. Her desire to serve others and her kind heart is any parent's dream. "Daddy, I love the potato-sack-rides to my bed at night," she said of the over-the-shoulder-transportation to her bed every night. "Thank you Daddy for taking me to Dr. Mpaata. But she pricks my *bum bum*. When I cry, you hold me with your big hands. Daddy, you are handsome on the inside and the outside."

Tatenda *[tah-ten-dah]* is our boy and the second-born. At five years old, he is turning into a fine young man already. "The tackles are awesome!" he started. "I don't get nightmares, I sleep very well and no bed bugs come to bite. You said that I am responsible, you are showing me how to take care of the girls but Mama can be bigheaded. Thank you Daddy for coming home for lunch everyday, and sending me the post card from Cape Town. It was so cool, but Tumelo lost hers."

Finally, our littlest, Tumelo *[t-oo-mel-ow]*, who is three years old, concluded with the following, "I love when you come home for lunch. But Daddy, do not chase the *puss-nyaows* (stray cats that constantly raid our backyard) away. They are so cute. Don't forget to give me cuddles and kisses."

Not a mention of all the toys, books, trips, and candy we had bought them all year long. All that mattered to them were the relationships we had; everything else seemed irrelevant!

6. Pay it Forward

"You can't teach culture. You have to live it. You have to experience it. You have to share it. And most importantly...you have to show it."
—*Brent Harris*

Dream |drēm| noun • a cherished aspiration, ambition, or ideal

Dream Big

One video that I love to re-visit when given the chance is Season 6 of the show *America's Got Talent*. Not that I have set foot on American soil… rather, I can attend thanks to the TV and internet. One episode I am particularly fond of features a gentleman called Landau Eugene Murphy Jr. He was a fighter!

Landau was just a normal guy washing cars who wished that his journey had not been so rough. At nineteen, he was homeless and he thought he was going to die. But singing gave him hope. He met his beautiful wife and started a family. His winning number was Frank Sinatra's 'My Way.' Listening to his performance gives me goose bumps and brings tears to my eyes. His rendition is inspirational.

As he was declared the winner of the grand prize, one million dollars, his dream of sharing the stage with the legendary Patti Labelle came true. Together they performed Patti's 'You're all I Need.' What a beautiful performance it was. The magic, though, was at the end of the song. Patti held Landau's hand high in the air and told him, "Take your bow beau!" What? This was *Patti Labelle* taking a step back for Landau Eugene Murphy Jr. Not only did this act thrust him into the limelight, but Patti also quietly left the stage, allowing him to soak in his moment. Patti displayed that great humility.

Patti took this moment to pay it forward, to support someone who truly deserved a break in his life.

Becoming a responsible leader at home is possible. My wife and I have been privileged to have a firm grounding on parenting. When our mentors asked us to understudy them in a bid to help run some parenting classes, we were hesitant at first. What experience did we have to help us coach other parents on how to take leadership of their children's lives? We were young, with only two young kids at the time. Finally, after a lot of prayer, we took the opportunity and have never looked back. This is our fifth year, and we feel humbled with every new class we take on. In retrospect, my wife and I feel that we benefit as much (or more) from the class than our students do, as the experiences shared keep us in check with our own parenting. We have found out that as our children grow older, new opportunities and challenges continuously emerge.

Taking on a twelve-week class twice a year is no easy task. It is physically, emotionally, and spiritually draining. Many times we have felt like bailing out. However, for us this is a calling and a way to be of service to others who need a helping hand. We are paying forward what was so graciously extended to us by other angelic souls.

Over the years, I have encountered many parents and singles that have chosen to go down the road of proactive parenting. Initially, they were skeptical of their ability to take charge of their children and homes. Now they are in full control, enjoying the pleasure and company of their respective families. All it took them was a vision, the guts to make bold decisions, the courage to take responsibility for their future, and finally, the audacity to become the leaders they were destined to be.

Here, they share their experiences. What follows are the stories of Mr. W.P. Kamau (married father of three), Ms. Muthoni Njoba (single mother of one), Mr. Kasera Kadondi (engaged to be married), and Ms. Evelyn Wangari (single mother of one).

W.P. Kamau

My upbringing was typical of that of any middle class Kenyan kid in the 1980s. My father was the typical traditional breadwinner while my mother was more involved in the care and nurture of the children. My father was in the construction industry. His busy schedule and heavy work commitments meant that he left home very early in the morning and usually arrived back home around 7:00 P.M. This went on for the better part of my primary schooling.

Our household subscribed to a strict structure where the kids were confined to studies every evening between 7:00 and 9:00 P.M.

Looking back, I think this arrangement was functionally effective, but on the converse, emotionally inert. Since we went to bed immediately after our study time, we rarely had any opportunity to spend time with our parents during the weekdays. However, I am still in awe at what my parents – and particularly my father – managed to achieve for the family economically, while maintaining stringent order in the family.

The serious side effect of this order is that real and healthy relationships were never developed between our parents and me and my siblings. To this day, we are very successful in our various undertakings, yet we do not engage each other at a social level. Whenever my family meets at any social gathering, it is normally characteristic to find ourselves making excuses to leave early. We never had the chance to develop any friendships within our family.

This situation led me to personally seek to learn more about parenting. I did not want my family to have the same level of emotional inertness that I grew up in. I projected thirty years into the future when I would be about seventy years old. Would my children avoid my wife and I? Would they visit only when under dire circumstances or because it was a compulsory family function? In addition to this disheartening imagery, I have witnessed the following when I have observed my peers, and society in general:

First, with increased access to diverse information, children are much more knowledgeable now than when I was growing up. Today, the parent-as-boss to child-as-underling type relationship of the 1980s will not survive the collegial dynamics being introduced into the family framework. The flip side of this increased access to information at a very early age may over-expose our children, be it in sex, pornography, drugs, alcohol, or other vices. The fear of losing one's child to these vices is very real, not to mention the peer pressure they face.

In view of the above, I realized that I was not armed with the skills to parent in the twenty-first century. I needed to understand how successful parents were navigating these murky waters and ending up with their children becoming credible and well-adjusted citizens. That is when my wife and I opted into a ten-week parenting class run by two couples. This was an extremely eye-opening experience. It contextualized the reasons why adults end up with a specific personal brand thirty years on.

The parenting class answered my questions about why I had a specific outlook or default attitude regarding life. In jest, my friends often make assertions that my *OS* (operating system) requires an upgrade. Allegedly, that *OS* is very conservative and, reportedly, rigid and resistant to any upgrading. The parenting sessions brought to light how my upbringing had shaped my character. I loved my rigid *OS*, however I soon realized that I could not be the same type of father to my daughters as my father was to me. My default *OS* had fundamental and dangerous flaws. It was guaranteed to end up with girls who will not be my confidants, which is not the goal that I seek in my relationship with them.

When I project into the future, I see my daughters regularly visiting my wife and I with their families. I see us having fun together, and supporting each other in times of need. In the present, I would love for that to happen with my kids and their grandparents. Sadly, much as I may try and force it, it is an effort with little hope of success. To contemplate this is too depressing, as the outlook is not very promising.

During the parenting class, the facilitators displayed their proactive parenting approach when introducing their children. It helped that Kimunya and his wife would attend the 6:30 A.M classes together with their three young children. What struck me about their young children was that they were well behaved and orderly in their interactions with each other and the people they met. Immediately, I made a mental note that this was the vision I had for my little girls. The knowledge regarding the parenting process that had the greatest impact for me was the fact that you reap what you sow.

As the class progressed, my fellow parents shared the details of their relationships (or lack thereof) with their own parents. It was evident that the parents who consciously chose to be involved in their children's lives ended up having closer relationships with their children in their old age. Because of the class, I have now made a conscious decision to spend more time with my daughters. For example, I am now always at home before 6:30 P.M. in order to spend at least one-and-a-half hours with them before they go to sleep. I will spend time with each girl, making sure to do something specific that will help develop our relationship. Together, we work to build various memorable moments that we can reflect on as we change over time.

The parenting class put in perspective my role in the home, and approach to disciplining our children. It is interesting that having two girls–as well as my weight tipping the scales at 220 pounds (100 kilograms) – I easily default to *protector-in-chief* as opposed to disciplinarian for our children. My wife previously shouldered the burden of the disciplining since I could not bring myself to upset my relationship with the girls. The class gave me a rude awakening. As head of the home, I could not delegate the disciplining process to my wife. I had to be at the forefront of this battle. Therefore, I took steps to define and isolate negative behavior, to separate the culprit from the others, to discipline them appropriately for their wrongdoing, to teach the lesson and elicit apologies, and finally, to reconcile with the child to restore the balance of our relationship to where it was before their transgression.

Instituting these steps has been transformational and life changing for me. We called it *invoking Chapter 5 of the parenting class*, referencing the section of the parenting manual that dealt with how to discipline our children. The transformation in our children has been amazing, and for me, it brought perspective about instilling order in the home.

Nowadays, I am still the fun daddy. However, when need arises, we will also 'go upstairs' for a one-on-one training session with an errant child in order to get the girls back on track. Contrary to popular belief, they accept the pain that accompanies the discipline process. They appreciate the reconciliation, and they are even open enough to tell the other parent they were naughty and got a *chapa* (training spank) because of a certain ill behavior. I totally love it!

If I could concisely describe myself, I would say I was a boy's boy. I was comfortable with male bonding, conservative; I've always had a provider mentality, etc. When the invite for the parenting class was circulated within our friend network, I took the lead in pushing back, in addition to challenging its usefulness. I actually lobbied others to a mass picketing on the opening day to protest the inhumane 6:30 A.M. Saturday morning time slot. In retrospect, I say this with a lot of shame.

I have seen the direct link between active parenting and the formation of character, as well as the improvement of relationships between me and my children now, and in the future. I have listened to and observed as my peers struggle with raising their children, and I now have something to say to them. My sessions with my friends will never lack a ten-minute window when I talk to them about the benefits I derived from the classes and how our home has been transformed. I believe I am a better father to our children and a much better husband to my wife!

As we progress through life we continue to define our family charter, clarifying the things that the Kamaus do and do not do, building our set of values and the behaviors that constitute being a Kamau. I always get excited when I ask my daughter, "Are you a Kamau?" and she responds with "Yes I am!" or when I ask, "Do the Kamaus shout at each other?" and she promptly responds, "No we don't."

Parenting is a journey. We are taking one step at a time, and it is our dream that our children will look back later in life and say, "I want to parent my children just as Mummy and Daddy parented us!"

Muthoni Njoba

My son was born when I was just twenty-two years old, right after I graduated from university. I named him Lemayan, which means *blessed*. Looking back, I honestly thought I knew everything I had to know about motherhood. It was not long before I realized how desperately clueless I was. Here I was, a single mum who thought loving a child was enough to be a parent. But the cold reality is motherhood is not something you can freestyle your way through. A child needs structure, as well as a strong foundation of valuable lessons and memories that will shape their entire future of decision-making.

I decided to learn more about parenting because I got to a point where, although I recognized the kind of child I wanted to raise, I just did not know how to get him there. Being a single parent is tough and can be overwhelming. The one thing I was certain about was that God had to be the core foundation of everything I wanted to teach my son. Lemayan had just turned five years old when I enrolled in a parenting class and I thank God every day for the opportunity.

So what drove me to develop a vision for my family of two? I did not want my son to grow up struggling with insecurities, making negative decisions, engaging in rebellious behavior, or with a lack of a knowledge of God's amazing love and lessons. This had been my life and I did not want a similar lot for my young son.

When I was born, my mother was just twenty-one years old, while my father was twenty-seven. They were young parents intent in building their careers for the sake of their children, or so they thought. In the process, I did not have the opportunity to bond or learn from them in the critical first six-year window of my early childhood. As discussed in the parenting class, the first six years of any child's life are critical. This is the window that children learn how to respect authority. It is also the time that other valuable lessons are instilled, lessons that are essential to the development of the core values that will inform all of their future decisions. Learning this sparked a makeover of my parenting journey.

I am grateful my parents worked hard because they loved me and wanted to provide for me. However, I did not want to repeat the same mistake they made of being career-driven while neglecting to spend valuable time with their children. Parents need to deliberately dedicate a lot of effort to be present and active in a child's upbringing. I have lived with the consequences of my parents' choices for my entire life. Due to the lack of my parents' presence when I was younger, I know how much harder life can get without a structured foundation for a child. In a world where youth are exposed to excessive negative external stimuli, it is very easy for them to slide down the wrong path.

This understanding was not sufficient. I knew I had to seek more direction and knowledge to mend the broken fences in my life. The parenting class I chose to attend was transformational. Interacting with the class facilitators and other parents was invaluable, while the lessons and program structure were so well put together! It was not a gloss-over event—discussions and lessons dug deep into the heart of matters. The facilitators shared real-life examples of putting into practice their choice to be intentional parents, while admitting to their weaknesses and mistakes. Engaging together with other parents was the most powerful interaction. Seeing the many mistakes that we make as parents (yet brush off as normal and acceptable) was identified as the major problem in our parenting techniques.

Having the facilitators point us in the right direction was such a relief. Many times, a parent like me will never admit they do not know how, or what, to do when faced with a challenge regarding their child. Sharing with other parents was not only therapeutic but also valuable; hearing how others would deal with a similar situation was a great way to share knowledge and boost each other's confidence. I am particularly grateful for the references to the Bible and God's Word about parenting. That was an essential piece to understanding how a child's future is dependent on the responsible parental effort and input into the child's life. Learning these lessons was an emotional and uplifting process, an eye opening and encouraging journey—one that I recommend to every parent.

I can confidently say there was a profound change in my life, mind, and behavior over the course of the parenting class. To begin with, I forgave myself for all the wrong decisions I made growing up. Being a rebellious child, everyone thought I was tough and hardcore. Yet this was really a broken girl's way to scream for attention. That same attention that I lacked in those critical first six years will haunt any child—and by extension, their family—for a lifetime. I grew up making my own rules as I went along, and I can guarantee those rules were not good at all. For many years I thought there was something wrong with me, as I could not understand why my parents did not realize how much I wanted them to be involved in my life.

However, there were a few good times too, despite the fact that they were few and far between. Some of the best memories I have with my family consist of time spent in airport lounges as we all waited to board a plane to or from holiday destinations. This was the only time we spent any quality time with both my father and mother.

Thank goodness for this parenting class. I came to understand that my foundation was unstable, and so it compromised my entire future. I learned so much about how the woman I am today was significantly influenced so early in my childhood years. This knowledge explained a lot of my insecurities and fervent efforts to cover up for my negative behaviors.

Today I stand as a confident single mother with knowledge of the dangers of being an absent parent. I now treasure my time with my son and no work, social event, or anything else can take that precious commodity away from me. I love to teach Lemayan life skills, to read from the Bible with him, and to continue to be a reliable source of comfort, strength, and wisdom for him. With a stronger understanding of God's word, I now appreciate more the blessing of being a parent, and I know what is expected of me. Time is much more valuable to my son than material things, so time is my gift to him every single day.

When parents do not understand how to raise a confident, caring, and God-fearing child, then the likelihood of raising an insecure, selfish, and rebellious child becomes greater. My insecurities growing up led to making wrong decisions, being easily influenced by negative things, and intentionally bringing a lot of pain and shame to my family. When a child decides that *any* attention is good attention, that is dangerous because they will do whatever it takes—even if that is risking their lives—to get that attention. I respect and value my parents so much. Over time, we have grown to love each other, and to enjoy each other's time yet this has been a process that has taken twenty-seven years!

I would urge all parents to prioritize spending quality time with their children and exposing them to God's magnificent love. Only then will they be sufficiently equipped to make the right decisions when they are faced with a challenging situation. They will do the right thing even when no one is watching. I only got to know God when I turned twenty-seven years old. I now want to give my son the honor and privilege of knowing God from the tender age of five. Imagine what greatness he will know by the time he is my age!

Kasera Kadondi,

Through my interactions with Kimunya, I noticed his dedication to God and his family as well. He had a young family and I started looking up to him as a role model of how a man should lead his family, both spiritually and in deed.

Through these interactions, I figured I needed a mentor through life. When I started going out with my fiancée, Valentine, what better couple would I have to emulate than Kimunya and his wife Harriette? This is the reason why I introduced the two to my fiancée.

My interactions with him and his family will definitely shape up the vision for my future family. I have learned that for one to lead his family, he has to do things that are in their best interests. Peer pressure not withstanding. I really admire how God and family are his central focus; he travelled with them and shares as many experiences with them as possible.

As a medic, I thought I knew all there was about education. He shattered that bubble when I encountered him home-schooling his children together with Harriette. That was a first for me, and since then him and his wife have made me more knowledgeable. I still have their cookbook that I am still using to sharpen my culinary skills!

I have actually grown so much under their tutelage, I had not just let you in on this but now I have. I really appreciate the role he plays in my life. When my fiancée asked me why I was looking up to Kimunya and his wife as my mentors, I just told her that all I had to do was fall back onto our relationship.

Evelyn Wangari

It was in October 2011 that I visited the Nairobi Chapel for the very first time, and my journey into intentional parenting began. Pastor Oscar Muriu and his wife, Pastor Beatrice Muriu, were running a series of sermons on *Planting Oaks of Righteousness*. My son was only seven months old at the time.

Flashback… When David was born, I purposed through prayer to commit him to the Lord just as Hannah in the Bible had with her son Samuel. The birth of my son saw the beginning of a wonderful journey but my passion for parenting was spurred on by *Planting Oaks of Righteousness*. Learning of my parental responsibilities from an in-depth spiritual perspective and acknowledging that God gives provision to all and equips them for every good work gave me more confidence to pursue parenting as a top priority in my life. Then I learned of an upcoming parenting class and promptly signed up for it.

Even before the February 2012 class, I was already acquiring Christian books that provided loving guidance on going about the parenting business. My zeal to be more family-oriented began to grow. I read books such as Elizabeth George's *A Mom After God's Own Heart*, Cynthia Yates's *Living Well As a Single Mom*, the Focus on the Family text *The Spiritual Growth of Children*, and many more. Although I am a single mother, I consider myself a parent just as any other. And as such, the parenting class for me was not about managing as a single mother, but instead I focused on being a parent who honors the Lord.

My course facilitators, the Kimunyas, were, and continue to be, such a blessing. I saw their passion for parenting in the way they shared their experiences in a practical way. They even defined it as their calling and ministry.

The ten weeks I invested in the class saw me become increasingly enlightened regarding the consequences of my choices. The very first session in the group was extremely profound because I learnt that obedient parents will most likely have obedient children. That statement alone made me carry out an in-depth analysis of my life, my choices, and the various mistakes that I have made. I knew there and then that I had to make my way right with God in order to effectively train up my son in accordance to His will. I did not want to be the parent that preaches water yet drinks wine. I wanted to be present and in right standing with God to be able to lead by example and influence my son in the right way.

This led to the realization that I committed too much time to my job. I seldom used to see and engage with my son. Working at a bank can be overly demanding, especially during a banking IT-system migration process. I would only see my son two days in a week because I always left for work while he was asleep and arrived back home when he was already in bed for the night. I never engaged with him and had no way of knowing how his day was.

At this point, I took the bold step and resigned from my job. My responsibility as a mother and homemaker was my topmost priority and I chose not to compromise it any further. I entrusted my future, and that of my son, into God's able hands. I knew that while I chose to faithfully pursue the priorities He ordained for my life, He would be faithful to lead me to the profession that would not compromise those very priorities.

So far, the journey has been an amazing blessing. Every single day is a seamless experience filled with learning. I still make mistakes, but I am thankful for each moment I have with my child. I learned the importance of setting standards in my home and ensuring that even my nanny follows them. During the class, I also learned how to go about training and disciplining my child. This experience can sometimes be overwhelming, and requires my sheer determination, as well as consistency in approach. I learned that children thrive on routines, so it is important to set a routine for the entire household to follow. However, I also soon realized the need for flexibility and learned to accommodate adjustments to the routine.

The Lord has been so faithful. I stayed out of work for only two months and was able to get a job that I appreciate even more, and actually enjoy. It was the perfect trade-off. To give up so He could lift me up and establish me. I would encourage every parent out there to pursue parenting as a top priority, and to participate in any solid opportunity to engage with other committed parents. If there is a parenting class you can plug into, do so by all means possible. Retake the class every so often as your children grow into different stages of life. Keep the passion for parenting burning.

Epilogue

"What we have done for ourselves alone dies with us; what we have done for others and the world remains and is immortal."
—*Albert Camus*

Without Forgiveness, Forget Effective Leadership

Nearly thirty years later, I chose to forgive my father. It had been a long, arduous journey, but one I had to take if I was to live my life to its fullest. I realized that if I was to become a leader to my own family—and beyond—I did not have any option but to forgive. When I hold back forgiveness, it becomes nearly impossible for me to build and nurture any relationship. Without a relationship, I can't lead anyone, as I will have no followers to lead.

I was reading Tanveer Naseer's blog post *Using New Year to Embrace Change and Failure*[33] and one particular section caught my attention. "The people you lead need to see that you're not simply reacting to what's happening around you, but that you're making sure you're ready to provide them with whatever support and opportunities they'll need to succeed. This is why leadership today is less about what you know and more about the relationships you have with those you serve as [they] need to see that you have their backs as much as you expect them to have yours. It's also why leadership is becoming harder to do well because it requires that we do more than simply maintaining the status quo, but that we seek out avenues and opportunities to improve things; to make things better both for those we lead and for those we impact through our actions."

With this in mind, on Christmas morning 2012, I called my father for the first time in five years. I have no recollection of the last time I spent Christmas with my father. This time, I called him just to wish him a Merry Christmas. And it felt good. My heart was not beating on overdrive, my breathing was normal—the chocker hold I had previously felt on my throat was gone! We had a very cordial conversation. For the first time in their lives, my children spoke to their grandfather. For the first time in his life, my father heard the voices of his two oldest grandchildren, and that of his fourth grandchild. For the first time, he could wish his grandchildren a

Merry Christmas. This was seven years after the birth of his first grandchild, my oldest daughter.

One week later, at 12:11 A.M. on the dawn of January first, my cellphone rang. It was my Dad on my first call of the year. He just wanted to wish me well in the year ahead.

Thirty years later, nearly to the dot, the healing began. For the first time in my life, I felt like I could stop running, and start living again. It was like blood supply was restored to some dead tissue in my body.

True Leadership Brings Restoration

If leaders can be ready to forgive others of any hurt or harm that has been directed at them, then restoration is an inevitable outcome. I can now work at restoring my relationship with my Dad without fear. When you allow true leadership to arise in you, you place yourself in a position to redeem your full potential to relate with other people.

Are you ready to lead from within? Consider this statement from a World War II survivor of the gas chambers. He had every right to be angry and vengeful of his captors. Yet he chose a different path and showed great leadership that can only come from the heart. "There is no need for wars or violence, under any circumstances. There are no problems that cannot be solved around a table, provided there is good will and reciprocal trust or even reciprocal fear."[34] Promo Levi, Auschwitz survivor.

Forgiveness and restoration started with himself before he could accept the same of others.

Show Passion

A passion to do what is right has mapped out my path to leadership at home, in the workplace, and in my community. This passion drives my commitment to provide my family with a solid identity. If my children cannot identify who they are, what they stand for, and where they are going, then what is the point of living? You will face opposition and ridicule from family, friends, and associates. What will give you skin thick enough to ignore this and push on?

"You need a lot of passion for what you're doing because it's so hard. Without passion, any rational person would give up. So if you're not having fun doing it, if you don't absolutely love it, you're going to give up. And that is what happens to most people, actually. If you look at the ones that ended up being successful in the eyes of society, often times its the ones who love what they do, so they could persevere when it got really tough. And the ones that did not love it, quit. Because they are sane, right? Who would put up with this stuff if you do not love it? So it is a lot of hard work and it is a lot of worrying constantly. If you don't love it, you're going to fail." Steve Jobs

Have a Giving Heart

A leader is called to give unreservedly. I have benefited from great people who have taken me under their wing and provided me with direction. My own determination to lead called for me to work hard, and to endure through change.

"Managers are numerous as the sands on the seashore, but leaders rarely wash up on the shore. While we believe recent worldwide events have highlighted the need for change in leadership style, ethics and attitudes, as a society we suffer from the cycles of failing due to consistency and the convictions to lead with the heart, soul and correct principles. Leading change has to start with me.

"Are there habits I need to change or establish, traditions I need to reconsider and leadership attributes I need to acquire or polish?

"If we are to raise a generation of leaders that are actively engaged and concerned with people more than profits, and society more than self, then I have to step up and make the change myself, and share my convictions, experience and knowledge with others. If I do this, then we'll notice the seashore is covered with leaders,"[35] Jim Holland.

Adventure in the Making

Parenting is an adventure, with vistas to enjoy and rough seas to navigate. I am learning that I need to enjoy myself more as I lead my family. My upbringing had primed me not to trust anything or take anyone at face value. I have always had all manner of possible scenarios worked out in advance, 'just in case' anything went wrong. I was dying from the inside. As I learn to change, I love the lessons from Aaron Brinker, a father of one son:

"*Laugh* – There are so many things in the world to make us sad. Instead of looking for sorrow, we should look for humor and things to make us laugh. Laughing at things makes our children and us happier.

"*Love* – One of the words I strongly discourage my son from using is hate. I will tell him it is alright to dislike something but hate is forever. I believe if someone says they hate something they have already made up their mind and I can't change their opinion.

"*Learn* – Parenting is a constant learning curve. The moment a parent decided they know everything is the moment they will fail. If a parent is willing to make a lifelong commitment to learning we can teach our children to become receptive to new ideas and new concepts.

"*Live* – Live each day to the fullest. Don't live with regrets and mistakes you have made in the past. If we make an effort to live in the present, our life will be richer and we can show our children about inner happiness." [36]

Allow Yourself to Innovate

To become an intentional parent, you have to develop your ability to become a leader in innovation. As a parent, I will often need to make adjustments on the fly. However, I have to constantly equip myself with the tools and knowledge required to innovate. I need to have the right attitude. Parenting is a calling, not a job.

"We're constantly focusing on innovating. We believe in the simple, not the complex. We believe that we need to own and control the primary technologies behind the products that we make, and participate only in markets where we can make significant contribution.

"We believe in saying no to thousands of projects, so that we can really focus on the few that are truly important and meaningful to us. We believe in deep collaboration and cross-pollination of our groups, which allow us to innovate in a way that others cannot.

"And frankly, we don't settle for anything less than excellence in every group in the company, and we have the self-honesty to admit when we are wrong and the courage to change."[37] Tim Cook, former Apple COO.

Full Steam Ahead!

What are your next steps? Are you going to take the lead at home?

Let me suggest that you start by establishing a solid heritage for your family. As Kent and Barbara Hughes point out, "Common sense, as well as research, tells us that a vital element for building a family is instilling a healthy sense if heritage, an appreciation of one's roots, both earthly and spiritual."[38] Essentially, it is important for your family to have an experience of coming from something of great ideal and to be bound by it.

Capture the moment and become the difference that this world so desperately craves. Ahmed Kathrada, a former prisoner at Robben Island, once said, "Someone has written about two prisoners looking out of their cell window: one saw iron bars while the other saw stars."[39]

For the longest time, being unable to forgive only made my life more miserable. All I could see were the bars that caged me from my freedom. Only when I chose to see the stars did I find the true freedom that has helped me to become better at serving others. It was seeing beyond the bars that made me realize that the bars were part of a gate. All I needed to do was unlatch that gate and walk towards the dream that so recently had been little more than a small hope hanging on a limb.

Live, Love, Matter...

"Authentic and transparent!"
–Barry Smith, Building What Matters

DOWN
BUT NOT OUT

BECOMING A SIGNIFICANT
LEADER AT HOME

| Workbook |

KIMUNYA MUGO

Down But Not Out: Becoming a Significant Leader at Home Workbook will help you to take leadership you have always wanted over your family.

Have you ever…
- Experienced hurdles that affect how you engage with or react to issues and circumstances at home?
- Lived with self-regret on relationships you had as a child that limit your capacity to lead at home?
- Struggled through the journey of self-discovery of how to lead at home?

What if you could…
- Work through wounds and difficult issues that hold you back.
- Find yourself celebrating joyous moments as you diligently apply what you learn
- Be the leader your home deserves.

Get a copy of the Workbook from…
www.leadbychoice.co

End notes

1 Oxford Dictionary of English

2 "Black Beauty," *Wikipedia*. Last updated September 10, 2013. http://en.wikipedia.org/wiki/Black_Beauty (September 23, 2013).

3 Anna Sewell, *Black Beauty* (London: Harper Press, 2010).

4 John Eldredge, *Wild at Heart: Discovering the Secret of a Man's Soul* (Nashville: Thomas Nelson Publishers), 106.

5 Malcolm Gladwell, *The Tipping Point: How little things can make a big difference* (London: Abacus, 2010), 141.

6 Henry Cloud and John Townsend, *Boundaries* (Grand Rapids: Zondervan, 1992)

7 John Rosemond, *Parent Power: A Common-Sense Approach to Parenting in the '90s and Beyond* (Kansas City: Universal Press Syndicate Company, 1990), 20.

8 Dr. Kevin Leman, *What a Difference a Daddy Makes: The indelible Imprint a Dad Leaves on His Daughter's Life* (Nashville: Thomas Nelson Publishers, 2000), 72.

9 New International Version, International Bible Society

10 New International Version, International Bible Society

11 Sidney Poitier, *The Measure of a Man: a memoir* (London: Simon & Schuster, 2000), 56-57.

12 John Eldredge, *Wild at Heart: Discovering the Secret of a Man's Soul* (Nashville: Thomas Nelson Publishers, 2001)

13 Michael Hyatt, *Creating Your Personal Life Plan: A Step-by-Step Guide for Designing the Life You've Always Wanted* (Nashville: Michael Hyatt, 2011)

14 Bruce Cockburn, *Lovers In A Dangerous Time* (Produced by Jon Goldsmith and Kerry Crawford. From the LP "Stealing Fire", 1984)

15 Irene Becker, in One-Degree Past Mediocrity, http://leadbychoice. wordpress.com/2012/04/15/one-degree-past-mediocrity/#comments

16 Greg Johnson & Mike Yorkey, *Daddy's Home: A Practical Guide for Maximizing the Most Important Hours of Your Day* (Wheaton: Tyndale House Publishers, 1992), 50.

17 Jay Elliot, *The Steve Jobs Way: iLeadership for a New Generation* (New York: Vanguard Press), 117.

18 James Baldwin, http://www.goodreads.com/ quotes/18154-children-have-never-been-very-good-at-listening-to-their

19 Wikipedia, *Gorilla* http://en.wikipedia.org/wiki/Gorilla

20 Garry & Anne Marie Ezzo, *Growing Kids God's Way: Reaching the Heart of Your Child With a God-Centered Purpose* (Louisiana: Growing Families International, 2007)

21 Anzaya & Mbithe Akatsa, *Parenting 101: The Kind of Parent God Expects You to Be*

22 Gary & Anne Marie Ezzo, *Growing Kids God's Way: Reaching the Heart of Your Child With a God-Centered Purpose* (Louisiana: Growing Families International, 2007)

23 Peter Mutua, *Lack of role models harms business and society* in Business Daily November 20, 2012 (Nairobi: Nation Media Group, 2012), pg. 29

24 Malcolm Gladwell, *Outliers: The Story of Success* (New York: Little, Brown & Company, 2008)

25 Andrew Carnegie, *The Road To Business Success: A Talk To Young Men,* From an address to Students of the Curry Commercial College, Pittsburg, June 23, 1885. (http://www.historytools.org/sources/ carnegie.html)

26 Oliver Van DeMille, *A Thomas Jefferson Education: Teaching A Generation Of Leaders For The Twenty-First Century* (Utah: George Wythe College Press, 2006), 14.

27 Seth Godin, *Stop Stealing Dreams* (Self-published e-book) pg. 61.

28 Mortimer Adler, *Teaching, Learning, and Their Counterfeits* http://
www.cambridgestudycenter.com/teaching-learning-and-their-
counterfeits (Cambridge Study Center, 2013)

29 William Ellery Channing quotes, (http://www.goodreads.com/author/
quotes/949667.William_Ellery_Channing)

30 Morgan Freeman, in *Invictus* (Warner Bros. Pictures, 2009) based on
the John Carlin book *Playing the Enemy: Nelson Mandela and the Game
That Made a Nation*

31 Herbert L. Fred, The True Teacher, (http://www.ncbi.nlm.nih.gov/
pmc/articles/PMC2879191/)

32 Zig Ziglar, *Breaking Through to the Next Level* (Colorado Springs:
Honor Books, 1998)

33 Tanveer Naseer, *Using New Year to Embrace
Change and Failure* http://www.tanveernaseer.com/
using-new-year-to-embrace-change-and-failure/

34 Promo Levi, '*The Drowned and the Saved*', 1986.

35 Jim Holland, *Leading Change Based on Character in 'The LeadChange
Revolution: Instigating a Global Movement for Character-based
Leadership!* (San Francisco: LeadChange Group, 2010),

36 Aaron Brinker, *Parenting – Life's Simple Pleasure* (Blog) *http://www.
dadblunders.com/2012/10/11/parenting-life-pleasure/*

37 Jay Elliot, *The Steve Jobs Way: iLeadership for a New Generation* (New
York: Vanguard Press), 226.

38 Kent & Barbara Hughes, *Common Sense Parenting: The essentials
of building a Christian Family!* (Wheaton, Illinois: Tyndale House
Publishers, Inc., 1995), 3.

39 Ahmed Kathrada, *Letters from Robben Island: A Selection of Ahmed
Kathrada's Prison Correspondence, 1964-1989* (Cape Town: Zebra Press,
2000).

About the Author

Kimunya Mugo is a communication specialist, with a passion for family, authentic leadership and branding. Kimunya writes a blog, *Lead by Choice,* and has been a parenting coach since 2007 together with his wife Harriette. They have three children and live in Nairobi, Kenya.

Notes

Notes

Notes

Notes

Notes